Robert Campbell Moberly

An account of the question which has arisen between the Bishop and the Church Missionary Society in the Diocese of Colombo

being a paper read originally before the Oxford Missionary Association of Graduates

Robert Campbell Moberly

An account of the question which has arisen between the Bishop and the Church Missionary Society in the Diocese of Colombo
being a paper read originally before the Oxford Missionary Association of Graduates

ISBN/EAN: 9783744741385

Printed in Europe, USA, Canada, Australia, Japan

Cover: Foto ©Lupo / pixelio.de

More available books at **www.hansebooks.com**

WHICH HAS ARISEN BETWEEN

THE BISHOP

AND THE

CHURCH MISSIONARY SOCIETY

IN THE

DIOCESE OF COLOMBO

BEING A PAPER READ ORIGINALLY BEFORE THE

OXFORD MISSIONARY ASSOCIATION OF GRADUATES

ON *FRIDAY, OCTOBER* 20th, 1876

AND SINCE COMPLETED

BY

ROBERT CAMPBELL MOBERLY, M.A.

Senior-Student of Christ Church
Chaplain to the Lord Bishop of Salisbury

Oxford and London

JAMES PARKER AND CO.

1876

OXFORD:
BY E. PICKARD HALL AND J. H. STACY,
PRINTERS TO THE UNIVERSITY.

PREFACE.

In case this paper should pass beyond the circle of those for whom it was originally drawn up, it is perhaps right that I should add a few words in explanation of myself and of my writing. The explanation is simply this; that I happen to have exceptional means of doing what I believe is urgently required to be done. I was one of those who, with the Bishop of Colombo, in the early dawn of the last Epiphany morning,—dropped from the docks out into the Thames, for the voyage to Ceylon. I landed with him in Colombo early in February; and from February till the last day of June (though not always, nor even generally, in the Bishop's company) I remained continuously in the Diocese. And again in the middle of August, when the events of July were all finished, but still fresh in memory and conversation, I landed in the island, and stayed in Colombo for a further week. These facts must be my justification for writing at all.

One other word of preface may be seemly. I trust it will not be thought that I mean to speak of those Clergy, with whose names I have had to deal, with the smallest bitterness or exultation; may I venture rather to express to them (if it be not too great a liberty) my respect for them; and to commend my account to their friendliness; and hereby to beg them all—both Mr. Jones (with whom I greatly rejoice to feel that I may claim acquaintance), and his colleagues, whom I have met, or whom I have not met,—to pardon the bluntness of my apprehension, if there be anything in this paper which may seem to their judgment to be untruly or unkindly said?

I. The Nature of the P...
cumstances of the...
landed in Februa...

II. Its First Developme...

III. Correspondence with...

IV. Mr. Clark's Policy i...

V. Interview with the C...
July 11

VI. The Principles in Qu...

VII. The Right Apprehen...
plicated by an imp...

VIII. Proceedings during t...

IX. Subsequent Modifica...

X. Conclusion

AN ACCOUNT, &c.

I AM to give an account of a question which has arisen in the Diocese of Colombo, and which is still in dispute. A question in dispute implies two sides: and when it is known that on the one side stands the Bishop of the Diocese, your own friend, very familiar and much looked up to in this place, and on the other side a body of Clergy, Priests and Deacons in the Church of Christ, respecting whom the one patent fact is that they have devoted their lives to the preaching of Christ among the heathen, you will hardly be satisfied with any account which is content to represent or regard the position of either side as unnatural or as inexplicable. Rather it will be part of my task to try and show how reasonable, at least in a certain sense, is each of two incompatible contentions. I advisedly say how reasonable, and how intelligible: because if bound on the one hand to try and understand both sides alike, on the other hand I do not wish to slide into that easy method of retrospective justice, which is apt to assume that if two disputants are both respectable, and their contentions both entirely intelligible, therefore both must be right, or to speak more exactly, therefore neither can be right. At the same time I am not going to talk about right and wrong: but to show, if possible, what is the question of principle at issue: and what are the considerations and actions which have created the situation. And please distinguish these two. There is a question of principle, at which we shall arrive presently: and there is a history of things hoped, and things feared, and acts done, all of them with their consequences trailing behind them,—seeming to affect the question of principle,—certainly affecting the relations, present and prospective, of individuals in Ceylon: but while the history is undoubtedly complicated and difficult, the principle, if I rightly understand my own story, is simple and clear.

To explain the facts, as I understand them, I must go back to the very beginning. The Bishop of Colombo, as you know well, resolved himself to be a missionary, before he was selected by others to be a Bishop. Naturally therefore, when he went out from hence to be Bishop of a diocese containing hundreds of thousands of heathen, the missionary ardour and hopes filled his thoughts and kindled them more than the more immediate duties of Diocesan administration: or perhaps I should put it thus,—the ideas of Diocesan administration and organization shaped themselves with a certain reference to the more absorbing interest of missionary work among the heathen. Again, the Bishop of Colombo, as you know well, has direct natural interest, as scholar and linguist, in the study of languages; and therefore the more, when he was on his way to be a Bishop in a heathen land, full of the awe of the prospect, and not as yet buried in daily businesses, the natural ardour towards the heathen took the form of ardent diligence in their language. Ardent earnestness heathenwards,—an earnestness whose preliminary expression was earnestness in the study of the native customs and languages; this I believe to have been a feeling strong within him, as day by day we drew nearer to Ceylon. And what he felt for himself, that he felt for others also. Earnestness towards the heathen, earnestness whose preliminary necessity was the study either of Tamil or Singhalese;—this seemed to him to be the one intelligible meaning and rationale of the lives of English Clergy brought from England to live in the midst of Tamils and Singhalese. One or two such he had brought with him already: many more he hoped to receive in course of time. What could be more self-evident than this, that the first preliminary with everyone must be the learning of Tamil or Singhalese? He had not brought them,—he would not I suppose have succeeded in getting hold of those he had brought,—but that there was work to do in proclaiming the gospel of Christ to those who knew it not: and in like manner for the future, he could not with any hope of the highest success, and most assuredly he would not, appeal to young men to spend their lives as ministers of Christ in the midst of heathen, and yet at the same time separate utterly from their motives in coming out, and from their lives in Ceylon, all missionary interest, all ministerial contact with the natives who would surround them. This, then, was to him the most obvious of obvious truths: Earnest men cannot live, as Christ's ordained ministers, with heathen swarming round them every day, without doing their best to be—in different degrees,—but all, and of course, in some degree, missionaries; without therefore trying, if possible, to learn their neighbours' language, in the express hope of being enabled to win them from darkness to light. I remember very well, during that time of coming near to Ceylon, with what strangeness an echo of the contrary assumption struck across us. A fellow passenger was speaking in the way one knows well, disparagingly and incredulously, of the use of Chaplains. Some word was said—(by accident certainly, for there was no suspicion that any word was needed)—about the effect that must surely follow from a man's getting into talk again and again with the coolies; and forthwith at the idea of a Chaplain's getting into talk with the coolies, our friend's whole manner of speaking on the subject was changed. The obvious novelty of the conception, the way in which it had plainly never even occurred to him that a Chaplain might learn Tamil and occupy himself with Tamils, took us not a little aback. One hardly knew whether to laugh or to cry. We did not indeed suppose, because one planter had never thought of it, that therefore no Chaplains ever did learn the language; but it was perplexing enough to find that any man could spend years in Ceylon, and retain such a notion of the functions of English Clergy.

Thus then for himself, for those who had come out with him or were to come out to him, and as far as possible for any who might have entered already on clerical life in Ceylon without it, this earnest yearning heathenwards, this earnestness whose preliminary necessity was study of language, seemed to the Bishop the first condition, indispensable to the usefulness of English Clergy if they were to spend their lives in the midst of heathen ignorant alike of English and of Christianity. This is the first point upon which I desire to insist. Be good enough to remember it in these two respects: first, that this was, in fact, the Bishop's mind on the subject, when he came to Ceylon; secondly, that it was in his mind, as I have tried to represent it, not as a balanced and hesitating opinion, but as obvious matter of course, as a sort of truism, selfevident, preliminary to everything.

And yet this simple fact, just so, by itself,—the fact that the Bishop desired that the Chaplains, and the Clergy who came out with or to himself, should learn the vernacular, and try to influence the heathen,—contains in itself the germ out of which a large part of the subsequent troubles grew. This statement, baldly made, sounds to me a startling one; and I wish it to sound so to others.

Now, then, let us ask how it could come to pass, or what it means, that so obvious a desire on the Bishop's part could be the cause of any distrust or dispute?

First, it is easy to answer that the circumstances were such, that a Bishop coming out with the expressed desire to make the Clergy round him, and the Chaplains, all take some part in missionary—and especially in Tamil missionary work, seemed to be threatening, and (as things stood) to be coming out with the direct design of threatening, the position previously occupied by others. So much I suppose would have been the case with any Bishop who should have come to Ceylon with such an openly expressed desire. But add further to this that the

Bishop, still personally unknown, was reported as very young, very enterprising, very High Church, and that the Clergy who accompanied or were to follow him were said to be young also, High Church also, and numerous,— a compact company from a High Church University, and that those who occupied the field already were exclusively Evangelical: and I believe I should not be wrong in saying that there were those to whom the whole thing seemed as an organized plan for ousting the Evangelical party from their work, seizing upon their missions, and handing them over bodily to Ritualists.

I am far from wishing to imply that all this was from the first the deliberate belief of the Clergy of the Church Missionary Society. It is a description of the very extremest, not the ordinary, interpretation put upon things. But I believe that even in its extremest form the suspicion had some existence: and I believe that there was a good deal of uneasiness, not amounting to this or anything like this consciously, yet tending towards the same direction, and (as it gradually formulated itself) growing, even in naturally sympathetic hearts—so far as in hearts naturally sympathetic it could grow—towards a result like in kind to this. I have struck the main chord, and meant to strike it, somewhat roughly,—rudely if you will: but I believe that the strains of thought and feeling in many men, though not rough but gentle, were nevertheless vibrating in this key.

But all this is but an imperfect answer to the question. If the circumstances were such as to make a fear like this natural, or in any sense reasonable: it is necessary to understand the circumstances with some plainness. At the risk of repeating facts familiar to many, I must endeavour to describe them.

What I have said hitherto I have said of Ceylon in general, and it applies, with more or less directness, to the Clergy throughout the island. But since it applies to one part more directly than the rest, and to that one part belong all the more important events that followed, we may now confine ourselves to that. There is a *mountain* country in the Diocese, and there is a *low* country: to the *low* country belong most of the Church Institutions, and most of the Church work,—almost all the Government Chaplains, almost all the work of the Church Missionary Society proper, which is mainly among Singhalese, all the work supported by the Society for the Propagation of the Gospel: but the whole of these we may for the present leave aside. Our present point is to understand what was, in February last, that condition of Church work in the *mountain* country, which caused the report of the Bishop's somewhat obvious aspirations to be received, not with enthusiasm, but with alarm.

First, then, as I suppose is very well known, the mountain country means the coffee-planting country: and the coffee-planting country means a country covered with large estates, on each of which there live, I suppose, some three or four Englishmen, and several hundred coolie labourers, who are Tamil immigrants from the South of India. I much regret that I am without statistics, and must speak in general terms. But at least we may take it, that over so large a number of estates, the number of English planters is considerable, and the Tamil cooly population very large. At some six or eight points over the mountain districts there are stationed [1] Clergy, who are commonly called Chaplains. In some degree this title is misleading, inasmuch as it is better known as the title of the Government Chaplains in India, whose position is not identical with that of the planters' Chaplains in the Ceylon coffee districts. These Chaplains are not, like the Indian Chaplains, and like some Chaplains in other parts of Ceylon, simply Government servants. Or, to speak more cautiously, especially as I am without authorities, for the most part they are not so. The Kandy Chaplain, indeed, who, though within the coffee country, is really a town Chaplain and not a hill Chaplain, is I believe in the fullest sense a Government Chaplain. And at least in some other cases, perhaps in most, the Government contributes a part of the Chaplain's salary, retaining I do not quite know how much or what kind of control over the Chaplain in consequence. But this Government contribution does not maintain [2] the Chaplain. It comes rather as an endorsement and encouragement of private efforts. The larger part of the income, at least in some cases I think the whole income,

---

[1] I speak as though there were actually at this moment Chaplains in all the Chaplaincies. Three or four were, in fact, vacant a few months ago, and I believe they are not yet all filled.

[2] In two or three instances, I understand, the Government contribution amounts to half of the Chaplain's income. I believe also that they contribute only to districts in which there is a Civil Servant stationed, in recognition of a public obligation to provide, as far as possible, religious machinery for public officers. May not this be said to be the principle upon which the whole system of 'establishment' in India and Ceylon is based?

is raised by the planters: and the Chaplains so provided by the planters are provided no doubt primarily for the planters' benefit. Let us take then the average Chaplain to be an English clergyman, maintained mainly by the contributions of English planters, and having his duties primarily towards them. He is, I believe, also generally appointed by the Bishop, and at all events is looked upon as being one of the more strictly Diocesan or Bishop's Clergy, in contradistinction to those who, though they are Clergy of the Diocese, and as such subordinated to the Bishop, are organized and governed under the direction of a Missionary Society. Our specimen Chaplain, then, will be stationed in a particular place, living in a house very probably provided by the planters' contributions, having probably a little church, or it may be two or three little churches in different directions, raised also by the planters; and being the Chaplain of a certain defined district whose limits he can exactly show you on the map, having therefore under his ken a perfectly definite number of estates, representing a perfectly definite list of planters and planters' assistants. They are, so far, a fixed clergy with geographical limits. Whilst there are but six or eight of them in the whole mountain country, their districts are large. The Chaplaincy which I know best contains four separate groups of estates—districts, as they are commonly called, each with its separate geographical name, each district containing several estates, I can hardly tell how many,—let us say half-a-dozen. Three of these four districts have their own little churches,—three churches at intervals of ten or twelve miles from each other: in the fourth district service is held once a fortnight in a private bungalow. Such then is our friend the hill country Chaplain, and the nature of his position and work. Two things, however, I think I should add to the picture, and perhaps I may add them here:—first, that though his 'parish' is so large that he can only reach half the number of his churches every Sunday, and can only be once every alternate Sunday in each, yet such is the nature of his 'parishioners' and their daily employment, that it would be very difficult—I should think impossible—for an active and earnest man to find adequate ministerial employment amongst them for his[1] week-day mornings, afternoons, and evenings:—and secondly, that all over his district he will see clustering, at intervals, the settlements of the coolie servants of these his 'parishioners;' there may be two or three sets of coolie lines within two or three miles; in one place at all events I have further seen a little native village within 100 yards of the Chaplain's house.

But while Chaplains are supposed to live thus, and with this employment, amongst the hills; there is a separate machinery, absolutely unconnected with the

[1] Even if he spends most of his nights as guest in successive bungalows (perhaps the most effective way of coming to intimacy with the planters), he will still have many more leisure hours every day in his host's absence, than are needed for riding to the next estate: and still there may, and probably will, be schools on the estates, which either he, or others from a distance, must visit and help: still the sight of the coolies will challenge his interest and effort every day: he can be learning their language; and even before he knows it, or knows more than a very little of it, he may be a real power with them, through native subordinates drawing their inspiration from him. If Chaplaincies were worked thus, I do not believe the average tenure of them would continue to be very short.

Chaplaincies, by which attempt is made to reach the Tamil coolies. The name of the Tamil Cooly Mission is well known: but we must say one or two things about it. First, it is a single organization, not at all parcelled out into independent districts, but preferring to deal with the entire Cooly population as one whole. Secondly, so far as the Church of England is concerned, and I believe so far as Dissenters are concerned also, it has the entire field of Tamil Cooly work in its hands: there is no other machinery besides it. Then as to its constitution: it has been often said that it has a mixed or unsectarian character. It is not unimportant to notice exactly how far this is true; for if it is partly true, it is certainly partly false. The contributors are Christians of various denominations: and they entrust their contributions to a Committee composed again of Christians of various denominations, including two or three Dissenting ministers. What then do the Committee do? They apply to the Church Missionary Society. They have collected such and such sums for the teaching of Christianity to the coolies. They ask the Church Missionary Society to undertake this work for them, putting themselves into the Society's hands for the execution of the work, and promising to impose no conditions which may fetter the consciences of the Society's clergy. The Society appoints accordingly one of its own clergy to superintend the Mission, and he is the responsible head, all subordinate workers, ordained or unordained, depending properly on him. There are surprisingly few clergy in the Mission. The Superintendent has only one English subordinate, and only, I believe, two or three ordained Tamils. I greatly regret that I can nowhere put my hand upon the authorized report of the Mission, and cannot therefore give full details in respect of the catechists and schoolmasters. They are, I have no doubt, numerous[1]: and many, perhaps most, of them are supplied to the Cooly Mission from the Church Missionary training school at Palamcottah. With reference then to the view that the Mission is unsectarian or dissenting in character, it is to be observed, that though the Mission is represented and its funds collected and given out by an undenominational Committee, yet the work of the Mission is not therefore undenominational, so long as the Committee adhere punctually to their principle of delegating all teaching work to the Church Missionary Society. It will prove itself to be in fact undenominational or otherwise, according as it is found, in fact, that the Church Missionary Society's agents do or do not work freely, in genuine independence of control, direct or indirect, from the Committee.

So much for its constitution:—now another point as to the way in which it is officered. I have said that there are surprisingly few clergy, and amongst them only two

---

[1] In the general report of the Church Missionary Society for 1874-1875, I read: 'The present staff of this Mission consists of two European Missionaries, a Native Assistant Missionary, a Native Pastor, twenty-three Catechists and Readers, fifteen School-teachers, and twenty unpaid Native Lay-assistants. .... There are also thirty-five schools, which are under the superintendence of the Mission, though supported from other sources .... The number of estates subscribing to the Mission has risen from 95 in 1873 to 194 at the commencement of the present year. The Native Christians number 936, of whom 242 are communicants; and there were 24 adult baptisms during the year.'

English clergy. Each of these two is superintendent and central administrator of an entire half of the coffee-planting districts. It follows from this, that, whatever their capacity to influence the whole country-side through their wise superintendence of others, their own personal contact with any individual district or estate must needs be slight and rare. An overwhelming proportion of the regular pastoral work must be done, and is done,—under them it may be, more or less remotely,—but immediately by others. These others are, in the immense majority of cases, unordained persons, catechists, or schoolmasters. The condition, then, even of a favorably circumstanced district will commonly be, that with the variation only of very occasional visits from a. clergyman, it will be shepherded by a catechist. The catechist will prepare catechumens for Baptism, and candidates after Baptism for Confirmation, will conduct services, will preach, will be in short in the place of a minister, performing at least nine times out of ten all the ministerial functions that are performed at all. The condition is in this respect somewhat as if a single clergyman *were set to superintend the rural Deanery of Oxford, and were to do this mainly by having a catechist for every group of three or four parishes, who should conduct all services (supplying the superintendent with various statistics, lists of congregations, reports of general progress, or of individual cases), the superintendent himself being acquainted with the district partly through the detail of these reports,—partly by means of such work as he was himself able to do as he went from district to district.

From its officering, we turn to a point which is important, as to its principle and method of working. This is its exclusiveness. I have said that it aims at embracing by a single organization the entire range of the coffee districts: and that it has the whole field in its hands,—there is no other machinery side by side with it. But this is not merely a fact concerning it: it is also a principle of its working, maintained with jealousy. When I say that it is exclusive, I particularly mean that it objects, on principle, either to share the Cooly work with other organizations, or to admit into its own organization workers independent of itself. I will ask you to consider this exclusiveness from two points of view. First, it is exclusive on Theological grounds. It is under the direction of a particular society, pledged theologically to a particular point of view: its agents, whether ordained or unordained, are chosen and authorized with reference to this theological stand-point: all the teaching of the Coolies is therefore based exclusively upon the Society's principles. These principles, I need hardly tell you, the Society regards as exclusively right; and thus it naturally follows that having the entire field of Cooly labour monopolized, in fact, in the hands of a distinctively Evangelical organization, the directors of the Mission regard the retention of the whole field under Evangelical teaching, as a matter of firstrate—I may perhaps say of sacred—importance. They are therefore peculiarly unwilling to tolerate any alteration which might have the effect of throwing a part of this field of work into the hands of clergy, who (though Priests and Deacons of the Church of England) yet are not Evangelical: or, to say the least, respecting whom the Society can have no security for their Evangelical doctrines. I trust it will not be thought that I am imputing motives or suspicions in this. I believe I am saying no more than has been said to me more than once, quite as avowed matter of principle, by some of those of whom I speak: and I have tried to shape the saying of it in a form which they might themselves not only admit but welcome.

But this exclusiveness has another meaning. It is maintained as necessary to the method of their working. The Tamil coolies are not settled inhabitants, but migratory,—brought up to the estates in gangs to meet particular engagements;—they may be here one season and out of the country the next: or they may be in this valley one season, and in the opposite corner of the coffee plantations the next. The heads of the Cooly Mission receive from their agents regular lists of the Christians in each district: (they are never, I believe, converted without being thus enrolled on the Society's books,) and so long as all the districts are under a single organization and report to a single centre, they feel that they have a power of following the movements of migratory gangs or individuals,—a power useful both for helping forward deserving converts, and for unmasking impostors,—which would be greatly impaired if responsibility were divided, and districts worked independently of each other.

I have spoken now of the attitude and circumstances of the two agencies for work under the Church in the mountain districts of Ceylon; and let me remind you again, that the entire area overspread by the somewhat wide-meshed network of the Tamil Cooly Mission which I have tried to describe, is identical with the area parcelled out into districts or parishes under the localized planters' Chaplains. One special result of the contiguity of the two I may here point out. It was sometimes the case that in one and the same place, there might be living side by side an English clergyman, resident as Chaplain, having no acknowledged relations with anyone but the English planters,—and a Tamil catechist ministering to a Tamil congregation, a Tamil schoolmaster teaching Tamil boys and girls, dependent both of them upon a mission-superintendent twenty or fifty miles away, but jealously independent of the Chaplain stationed in the place itself. Such a school I have seen in one place within twenty yards of the Church; which again was hardly more than fifty yards from the Chaplain's house:—all three close together, as in an English village; yet with the school and its master, with the catechist and his Tamil services, the Chaplain was allowed no connection. And having emphasized this, it would be fair to say on the other hand that there have, I believe, been individual instances in which the Mission authorities have allowed a Chaplain to take part in their school: and moreover that one feeling which has at least helped to intensify their reluctance to concede any more permanent footing to the Chaplains, has been their observation of the shortness and variableness of the average tenure of the Chaplaincies; so that Chaplain-management has presented itself as a precarious and unstable alternative to the steady continuity of the Society's organization.

Such was the general condition of things in the Ceylon hill-country, across which struck the announcement that a new Bishop, young, enterprising, High Church, with a band of Clergy like himself, were landing in Ceylon, bent before all things on this,—on learning, themselves, and inducing the Chaplains and all other Diocesan Clergy to learn the vernacular languages, in order that all might throw themselves with eager energy into missionary work. And I think I have said enough to show that such a desire, though from the other side so undeniable, so irresistibly self-evident, yet *was* calculated, as its announcement spread abroad through the island, not simply to evoke enthusiasm, but also, at least with many, to cause anxiety and grave foreboding. For it is plain that in the hill-country at least no Chaplain could learn a dozen sentences of Tamil; no Chaplain could lift his little finger to strive as the minister of Christ with the souls of Tamils, without having forthwith cut so far across the prerogative of an exclusive society, without having already awoke a complicated and far-reaching question.

All this we who were with the Bishop did not of course at all then understand : but the Clergy of the Tamil Cooly Mission understood it. The Bishop, I feel convinced, did not adequately understand it. I do not say that his principles would, or could, have differed a hair's breadth if he had appreciated it to the uttermost. But to him I believe his principle was, in the first instance, only the most self-evident of first principles—the most preliminary of truisms: and I can easily admit it to be more than possible that in the generous, undiplomatic, unsuspecting outspokenness which is his nature, he may have often spoken out upon this principle with a broad and sanguine joy, such as would rather widen than narrow the apprehensions of the missionaries, and such as a colder and more intricate soul than his, knowing of these apprehensions or fearing them, might have discarded as impolitic.

We have hardly yet got beyond the date of his landing: yet I believe that we have got in its essentials the whole position. Many details of act follow on both sides—wise or unwise: but they are but the outcome of this original condition, more or less wisely or unwisely handled. It is clear indeed that it would have needed great perfectness of wisdom on both sides to weld and smooth together two principles of action—both natural—both, it may perhaps be urged, inevitable, but too certainly incompatible with each other.

It is as well perhaps in the interests of brevity that I cannot follow with any detail the development of these questions through the earlier months. From the end of February to nearly the end of May I was only four days myself in the Bishop's company : and at that time I heard very little which bore upon the matter. I believe, however, that I should be right in general in saying that the Bishop on his part set himself from the first to one particular point in this connection, viz. to arrange that there should be no question about the Chaplains having some access to missionary work. He himself at a later date said that he had had in view from the first two aims in particular—'unity, real and not fictitious, and a missionary spirit in every clergyman;' or, as in a letter afterwards published, 'I have been for some time endeavouring to obtain a share in the work for the resident Chaplains.' I have no doubt that whatever in the way of compromise or partial concession he might have been contented with for the moment,—that which he really tried to work towards was an adjustment of the whole relation of Chaplains and Missionaries upon a sounder and more permanent basis: I have no doubt also that in conversation with Missionaries he talked always—as it would not be in his nature to decline to talk—with most perfect freedom and trustfulness of the principles upon and towards which he desired to work: and finally I do not now doubt that such conversations tended to confirm the suspicions of some of the Missionaries. An indication of this suspicion appears to show itself in a letter written by the Superintendent of the Tamil Cooly Mission (the Rev. W. Clark), as early as March 21st. After arguing with some detail that the Chaplains are very fully employed with their English work, he concludes argument and letter at once in these words: 'If the work which this implies is not enough, I am at a loss to think what is. No plea therefore for work among coolies can come from any alleged want of work. It must be derived from some other source. What that may be I leave to your lordship to consider.' The same gentleman, writing some months afterwards to the 'Colombo Observer' with reference to this time, says, 'The Bishop first gave intimation of his intentions with regard to the Tamil Cooly Mission to the Rev. J. Ireland Jones, in the course of a conversation with him *shortly after his arrival in the island*' (the italics are Mr. Clark's). 'Not long afterwards he spoke on the same subject to the Rev. A. R. Cavalier. Subsequently before leaving Kandy' [and therefore still in the middle of March] 'he spoke to me of it. All three Missionaries opposed his scheme on various grounds. I made notes of the conversation I held with him, and sent them to England for the information of the Committee of the Church Missionary Society.' This sending notes of a private conversation home to the London Committee appears to me important, at least as indicating how definitely at that time Mr. Clark thought it necessary to keep alert guard in the camp, watching the Bishop's indications of movement, as men would watch the movements of one who was thought to be meditating an aggressive campaign.

From the middle of March onwards the Bishop spent several weeks travelling through the coffee districts, and trying to make the way clear for interest and industry on the Chaplains' part, among their Tamil neighbours. One further thing, I have no doubt, began even in this first tour, to impress itself upon his mind, not as a condition of what he proposed, but as a new fact which experience showed him: and this was that the Tamil Cooly Mission work, as it stood, was an unsatisfactory and disappointing representation of the activity of the Church of England amongst the coolies. I can hardly say how definitely he felt this already in March. But this and his later visit in May together certainly caused him to feel it quite definitely, and in two distinct respects: first, because the meshes of the network were far too wide,—the catechists' visits to an estate were few and formal, and very ineffective,—the schoolmasters were too far from control to be brisk in their work, the Clergy were too few—the whole machinery in short was inadequate to the task: and secondly, because he had, little by little, increasing misgivings as to the practical influence, real even if indirect, exercised by the undenominational committee,—at the very least by the fact of the Mission's having an undenominational committee, and being supported more or less on the undenominational principle,—over the tone and manner of the teaching. It is to be remembered how large a proportion of this teaching was in the hands of unordained and unguaranteed catechists. He himself says a few months afterwards that during his 'short experience of the island, he has come across the cases of several catechists who have served both under the Ministers of some dissenting body and under the Clergy of the Church in turn, and has found that it was not always considered essential in a catechist that he should be acquainted with the special doctrines of the Church of England. This,' he adds, 'has made him the more conscious of the desirability of some guarantee of the orthodoxy of catechists.' I cannot fix the date of the realization of a new conclusion; but by degrees, certainly, through March, April, and May, he felt more and more that the Tamil Cooly Mission work was inadequate in its extent, if not dubious in its character; and he was therefore more and more deeply convinced that it was impossible for him, as chief pastor of the Church in Ceylon, to accept it, as it stood, as the full and sufficient discharge of the duties of the Church towards the large population of Tamil coolies. Meanwhile the Mission, on its side, clung with tenacity to its exclusiveness, little disposed [1] for con-

---

[1] I am bound in fairness to mention that there is one letter of Mr. Clark's about this time, that of April 5th, which seems to point to a different attitude from that which I have attributed to him. I have not introduced it into my account, for the plain reason, which I frankly own, that I could not clearly see its coherence with the things that went before and after, according to that interpretation which alone they have seemed to me to bear. But there is the letter; and I am bound to point to it, as evidence, so far as it goes, against my interpretation. The following is the passage in question:

'Still I would not have your Lordship to think that I am an obstacle to a zealous Chaplain's doing what he can for the coolies. I should

cession or compromise, but rather refusing and resenting any introduction of the Chaplains into that which it considered to be its own sphere of work. It is not to be wondered at if under these circumstances, before the months were ended, he had begun to realize with himself that the day must come when the entire organization of Church work towards the coolies would have to be remodelled, and the existing Cooly Mission, uncompromising, yet claiming monopoly, must either be transformed or disallowed. Little probably did he imagine that within so few weeks he would himself stand committed to a strong step towards this issue: but the issue itself I doubt not had begun to loom before him, as one which must sooner or later become inevitable.

Through all this time, though the difficulty of adjustment with the Tamil Cooly Mission was strongly felt, and was I suppose entered into by other Church Missionary Clergy in the island, there was not, I entirely believe, the very smallest hitch or appearance of difficulty between the Bishop and the Church Missionary Society in general. That his respect for some of them was most unfeignedly

welcome his assistance with pleasure. Anyone acquainted with the language may preach in my parish to the coolies as much as he likes, and if any planter wishes to place a school under his management, I shall not oppose any obstacles, but on the contrary assist him as much as I am able. But I cannot consent to give him any account of my doings, or to open my school to him, except as a friend, or to place the Catechists or other agents in any way under his direction, or to work the district as if I were there by sufferance only, and not in my own parish, or to allow the formation in it of separate native congregations.'

Even here, however, the standing offered to the Chaplain becomes, if scrutinized, rather foundationless and vague.

deep I know for certain. They on their part seemed—I doubt not genuinely—to be cordial towards him. It is only when, and in so far as, the Society in general begins to enter upon the Cooly Mission question, that there begins to be any fear of a misunderstanding between them and the Bishop.

WITH this, I suppose, we come to the next stage in the progress of things. It mainly consists of a correspondence (which has since been published) between the Secretary of the general Society, Mr. Oakley, and the Bishop. This correspondence belongs to the last part of May and the beginning of June. The first point upon which it hinges is the old difficulty, the adjustment of any relations between Chaplains and Missionaries in the coffee districts. The immediate occasion which gives rise to it is the near prospect of the ordination to Priesthood of two Deacons of the Church Missionary Society, one of whom is the Assistant Superintendent of the Cooly Mission. The occasion of ordination is the occasion also of licensing: and it is upon the terms in which the license is to be given that the correspondence first turns.

The correspondence opens with a letter from Mr. Oakley to the Bishop which I have not got, but my recollection of it is exactly expressed by Mr. Oakley's own description of it, namely, that it was to ask whether the Bishop wished that Messrs. Unwin and Cavalier should apply to him for licenses at once, in the middle of May,—or should wait till their time of ordination,—then less than a month distant. The Bishop replies that they had better wait:

'especially,' he says, 'as I must have some talk with them as to the limits of their work.' He goes on to say that his own wish is to give both licenses in the old undefined and general form of words, 'with the understanding that neither would enter on work within the sphere of another licensed Clergyman without his knowledge or consent, and that any dispute which might arise upon the limits of either's work, should be referred to me. It would be understood, on my part, that I should desire the localized Clergy to give the freest possible admission to the itinerant Clergy.' As an alternative—but a worse alternative—he suggests the possibility of defining exactly what places belonged to the fixed Chaplains, and what were still under the itinerant Missionaries,—the Missionaries in that case coming into the Chaplains' districts 'confessedly on sufferance.' Then, going back to principles, he goes on, 'I suppose it to be the aim of the itinerant Clergy gradually to produce localized Churches, with localized Clergy, and so by their own work continually to narrow their own field. This applies, I am aware, less fully to the Tamil Cooly Mission than to the Singhalese Itineracy. But,' he adds, 'you probably know that the Dimbola Chaplaincy is offered to Mr. Jones. If he accepts it, the problem of adjusting the claims of the so-called Chaplains and the Tamil Cooly Mission "solvetur ambulando."'

Mr. Oakley replied to this, representing that the Missionaries in both parts of the island always had received general licenses and worked without limitation; and that disputes had not, in fact, arisen. One limitation he himself proposed; or rather said that it already was accepted in practice: viz. that the Church Missionary Society should not interfere with any other Society, nor send its Missionaries where any other Protestant Mission was already itinerating. Otherwise he begged that their commission might be, as heretofore, without limitation. That ended the immediate matter and the first half of the correspondence.

But by this time the apprehensions of the Church Missionary Clergy were becoming too great for silence. Anxieties, as I have represented, had been growing from the first. The Bishop's conversations and letters had given at least some reality to these, and hints here and hints there, rumours from this side and from that, some true, some distorted or magnified, came dropping in. All were duly represented to the Church Missionary Secretary. He heard Mr. Clark's alarm as to the Bishop's intentions among the hills; he heard Mr. Jones' anxieties in Colombo; he heard of the Bishop's conversations with Mr. Cavalier about limits of work. Finally, at this particular moment, there was laid before him a note which Mr. Cavalier received just now from one of the Chaplains, which seemed to express in its plainest and ugliest form the whole of what the Society feared. It seemed to show that the Bishop was authorizing the Chaplains to treat the whole of the cooly work within their districts as their own. Mr. Cavalier had held a Tamil service in (I think) a coffee store in Dikoya. The Chaplain of Dikoya, writing to him, expresses his surprise that (to quote his own words) 'you did not write to me before coming into my district to hold service in one of my chapels. I have always understood it to be customary for one clergyman to write to another before going to his district to hold service, or in fact to minister even privately. I also regret extremely that you should have spoken to my men on the subject of the Bishop's interference, and more especially to the native Christians in my district, as I am most anxious that all under my spiritual charge should be loyal to their Bishop, and because I do not think it right that the term "interference" should be made use of to set them against that which the Bishop may be doing for the general good.' It will be observed, that if the Chaplain's claims are extreme, they were partly provoked by the perception that the missionary's exhortations were a little disloyal and dangerous.

I suppose that it must have been at the sight of this note that Mr. Oakley felt that the time was come to give up all indirectness and questions as to separate details, and plainly to challenge the Bishop at once as to this aggressive policy of his which the Society seemed to itself to have foreseen from the first, and to see now by little and little maturing itself and being carried into action. On the 1st of June therefore, not quite a fortnight after his previous letter, he wrote to the Bishop again. He wrote a long letter, setting forth in order the designs of the Bishop such as he now understood them to be. They amounted to this: that in all districts, whether Tamil or Singhalese, where there were Chaplains (who would distinctively be 'Bishop's' Clergy) the Bishop meant to transfer to these Chaplains absolutely the possession and control of the Society's work; the Missionaries were to appear only on sufferance, as their curates; the Chaplains were to control both the church buildings and all the services; were to prepare all catechumens and confirmation candidates; were to assume authority over the missionary schools; and finally to take out of the Society's hands the entire control of all catechists as well as schoolmasters, whom the Society had trained for its own work, and settled and wielded according to its own discretion. Having sketched out the plan in its different parts, Mr. Oakley proceeds to comment on each point separately, very temperately at first, though before the end it seems as if he hardly could retain his patience. Such was the letter which reached the Bishop on the evening of the 2nd of June.

Now in approaching the mention of this letter of Mr. Oakley's, I have tried to represent to myself and to you, how natural it was that he should feel as he did on the matter, and write as he did. I have tried to show (as far as it was possible that I should be able to see) how natural were the original anxieties; how naturally out of the original anxieties, coupled with an imperfect appreciation of what the Bishop really was striving after, grew the more developed condition of alarm; how naturally finally the immediate definite provocation[1] of Mr. Elton's letter, lying in black and white on his table before him, must have seemed to Mr. Oakley to force him into accepting as really true the whole rumoured purpose of the Bishop against the Society. But it must not be supposed that when on the evening of the 2nd of June the Bishop was looking anxiously

---

[1] I assume that he had seen Mr. Elton's letter before writing this. He does not himself refer directly to it in this letter, but does so in his next.

for certain much-expected letters from Oxford, and there came in instead—no English mail, but only Mr. Oakley's letter,—the Bishop knew, or could have known, all that had led up to this letter, and made it natural. He knew indeed of the hitch as to the terms of Mr. Cavalier's license: he knew of course also of the wider discomfort, so far as it was directly represented in the discussions about that; but he had been preparing a letter for Mr. Cavalier which he fully hoped, and as it proved justly hoped, would smooth over the whole of that immediate discomfort. Mr. Oakley's letter, ceremonious in tone, but in its statements reading like a long indictment, was to him I believe quite as much a disappointment, at a moment when he thought all hitches were being removed, as it must at any moment have been a distress.

The next day he wrote two letters, one to Mr. Cavalier, repeating again more precisely his meaning about the license, and one in direct reply to Mr. Oakley's letter. To Mr. Oakley he enclosed also a copy of what he had written for Mr. Cavalier. Of Mr. Cavalier's letter the most important sentence is that which defines the limitation of his work. . . . 'But I remind you that . . . the words "Southern district of the Tamil Cooly Mission" must be understood with limitations, since the area over which generally speaking that work extends, contains several places where are Clergy already holding my license, a license which authorises them to work among Tamils as well as other races. And the number of such localised Clergy may, and I hope will, hereafter be increased. So far as your work does not come into collision with theirs, it extends throughout their districts; but it is so far limited that it may not exclude the work—to whatever race directed—which they are licensed to do. The limitation is at present exceedingly small, and will not for some time to come be seriously felt; but it exists, and must be recognised. I do not ask you to be subordinate to any one but myself, nor to give to anyone a share in the organization and revenues of a particular society; only to recognise other Clergy as bearing their part in the work of building up the Church of Christ among the Tamils.'

In reading Mr. Oakley's letter, the Bishop had been surprised and pained at the many things which he found imputed to him; and in replying to it he aimed rather at soothing alarm, and restoring if possible mutual confidence (not forgetting indeed to disclaim in a sweeping manner the whole attitude attributed to him) than at taking the points one by one, and entering into defence or explanation upon each. Possibly—I do not know—he might have done otherwise, had he fully appreciated the deep seriousness of Mr. Oakley's suspicions; but this at all events was what he did. 'I am extremely sorry to think that I could ever have so expressed myself as to give rise to the apprehensions which your letter implies. I am as far as possible, I hope, from wishing to enter upon a course of such wild injustice as that which you describe; and you must forgive me for saying that I am somewhat hurt that so extreme a construction should have been put upon what I said. I must have spoken to persons already rather inclined to take fright. At any rate I spoke to those whose advice I valued highly, and if I did—though I do not remember it—propound any startling suggestions, I certainly did not threaten so violently to carry them out.

'However let me hasten to assure you that I will not, if I can help it, infringe the rights or thwart the efforts of the Church Missionary Society in any part of their work, a work for which I thought I had clearly shown my high regard and gratitude. There is not in my plans, so far as I know them, anything that I may not trust the good sense and loyalty of the Clergy to bring about as occasion requires; in my great desire to keep nothing in the background, I have it seems caused needless anxiety.'

He goes on to explain that the only point he insists on 'that is not clearly involved in the circumstances of the work' is 'Liberty to the Chaplains to minister to the Tamil coolies'; and that in case of any collision between the two agencies, the appeal must be to himself. 'Such a collision,' he adds, 'I am sure need never occur. I am quite prepared to trust the good sense of both parties to avoid it.' This was the character of his reply to Mr. Oakley.

The Ordination week was now just beginning. Happily the immediate point of Mr. Cavalier's license was, so far, settled. There were one or two conversations on the subject during the week, between the Bishop, Mr. Cavalier, and Mr. Jones; on that point, however, the different conditions were successfully harmonized; and Mr. Cavalier was examined, was ordained, and was licensed.

In the midst of the Ember Days came another letter from Mr. Oakley. It was not yet the direct reply to the Bishop's letter,—that was delayed, and this was written meanwhile. It was entirely upon the point of the relation of Chaplains and Missionaries in the coffee districts. In it Mr. Oakley quoted—what the Bishop had not before known of—Mr. Elton's letter; and also another reported order from a Chaplain to a Catechist, desiring that the Catechist should report himself from time to time to the Chaplain: he made strong representations against the subordination of Missionaries to Chaplains for Tamil work, rather than Chaplains to Missionaries; and finally requested the Bishop to reconsider the whole matter, and definitely to allow the Missionaries right of access to all coolies at all times. 'If,' he said, 'this be not conceded, the whole plan of the Tamil Cooly Mission must be changed, and the subject must be at once brought before the parent Committee of the Church Missionary Society, and before the friends of the Society in this island.'

Two days later, Mr. Oakley's real answer to the Bishop's letter followed.

It seemed that the Bishop's letter had taken just the wrong shape. The distrust was far too great to be removed by anything like general assurances. On the contrary, these rather deepened the general distrust. 'On each of these points,' Mr. Oakley says, 'I had hoped to be favoured with your Lordship's explanation. The letter with which you have favoured me contains merely a general disclaimer of hostile intentions towards the Church Missionary Society, which I am sorry to say is to me most unsatisfactory.' He says that he had been very reluctant to believe the reports which reached him of the Bishop's designs, but as they continued to come in from all sides,—

'all tending in the same direction—all leading to the same plan—shall I venture to say? despoiling the Church Missionary Society and supporting the position of the Chaplains. . . . I have most reluctantly come to the conclusion that the gentlemen above referred to have not misrepresented your Lordship's words, nor misunderstood your Lordship's intentions. And I am the more confirmed in this opinion by your Lordship's letter now lying before me.' This was because 'In every point but one the questions are left undecided. On that one point no doubt can any longer exist.' And presently he quotes the Bishop's words, 'There is one point on which I insist— liberty to the Chaplains to minister to the Tamil coolies,' and adds, 'Mr. Elton has shown very clearly what he understands by that "liberty," and this, I think, may be considered as a fair exposition of the whole question as it now stands.' And again, further on, 'Mr. Elton's letter *shows*, and your Lordship's remarks on the subject *show*, that the Chaplains are now placed in a position by which the future labours of the Missionaries may, at any time, be thwarted, and their efforts actually prohibited. And this your Lordship speaks of as "the liberty of the Chaplains," and which, you *insist* upon, *shall* be maintained! They (the Chaplains) are to be "*at liberty* to minister to the Tamil coolies;" the Missionaries are *not* to be at liberty to minister to them except with the Chaplains' consent!

'It is, I think,' he goes on, 'too much to suppose that the Church Missionary Society will silently consent to such proceedings. If they were to do so, what security would they have that their converts at other stations, and their agents anywhere and everywhere, would not also be interfered with, in strict accordance with the reports which have been circulated of your Lordship's wishes with reference to catechists, converts, native pastors, etc., as referred to in my former letter?

'Let me therefore respectfully request your Lordship to favour me *with definite replies* to these questions: (1) If it is your Lordship's intention to place our agents and our people under the care or control of Chaplains, wherever they (the Chaplains) may be located? or (2) If we may consider that we are at liberty, as formerly, to visit and instruct our people wherever they may be found, *without let or hindrance* from any of the Clergy in the island?'

It is useless, perhaps, to dwell upon the increased disappointment which this letter caused to the Bishop, when he found that the very words which he had intended to be all of peace and confidence, had only been taken by Mr. Oakley as 'most unsatisfactory,' as 'the more confirming' the extremest suspicions which were entertained as to his designs. The morning after the Ordination the Bishop left Colombo, to start on a tour along the southern coast. From the first halting-place on this tour he wrote to Mr. Oakley again. This letter I had better give almost in full:—

'PANADURE, *June* 12, 1876.

'Dear Mr. Oakley,—

'You will, I daresay, forgive my not answering your letter until the Ordination was over, especially as I have had opportunity of talking over some of the matters referred to with the persons actually concerned. I cannot be surprised that Mr. Elton's letter, and the story about the Pussellawa Chaplain, coming at the time they did, should have disturbed you; and I hope my disavowal of the principle contained in the former, and my condemnation of the conduct (falsely, I feel sure) attributed to the latter, will do something to restore confidence.

'Mr. Elton's claim to the "spiritual charge" of native congregations which the Tamil Cooly Mission have hitherto taught and collected and enrolled, is one which cannot be supported. He stands towards them much in the relation occupied by the Clergyman of one parish towards the parishioners of his absent neighbour—bound to do nothing, unless under urgent necessity, for which he has not the expressed or implied sanction of the pastor under whose care they are.

'I wish, for my part, that he should be admitted by the voluntary act of the Missionary, to a nearer relation; but without such voluntary act, he cannot, as things now stand, claim it.

'Mr. Duthy's orders to the Catechist are, I am pretty sure, fictitious. If not, they were utterly unjustifiable.

'I will next reply to the two questions of June 9th.

'(1) It is not my intention, and never was my wish, to place your "agents" under the control of "Chaplains;" nor do I intend to place your "people" under their care, unless with your permission. Some of the present misunderstanding has arisen from supposing that what I wished to see done by your voluntary act in a few cases, I intended to do, or attempt to do, without it, in all.

'(2) You are "at liberty, as formerly, to visit and instruct your people wherever they may be found, without let or hindrance from any of the Clergy in the island," except in so far as the Archdeacon, or any other officer hereafter appointed, may have lawful authority.

'I must now return to the questions of June 1st, though I think you should have been contented with my general answer.

'The "Missionaries" in the coffee-districts have the sole authority over their present congregations. The "Chaplains" have a right to form congregations or to open schools, and the "Missionaries" are not to thwart or oppose them; the "Chaplains" may also prepare candidates for Baptism, Confirmation, etc.; but the Missionaries alone have the right to prepare candidates from their own congregation.

'It is my wish that the Missionaries should enter no Chaplain's district without his knowledge. Should he protest against their entrance, I should, as a rule, require him to acquiesce; but should I find that the "Missionary" was actually hindering his work, I should request the "Missionary" not to enter that district. Such a case, as I understand it, is improbable in the extreme.

'(2) Catechists belonging to the Tamil Cooly Mission are not to be considered as in any way subject to the control of the "Chaplains;" but as I am bound to prevent one Clergyman from thwarting another, much more should I be bound to require the heads of the Mission to withdraw a Catechist who should oppose or hinder the work of a Clergyman.

. . . . . .

'These answers describe what I consider to be the present state of things, without implying that I think it, in every case, the best possible condition. I hope they are sufficiently distinct to allay suspicions which ought never to have arisen.

'The arguments advanced by Mr. Clark against my plan of enlisting in Mission work those Clergy who are appointed primarily for the English, have considerable weight; and that plan is still open to discussion, though I do not think I shall be persuaded to retire from my position of insisting on "liberty to the so-called Chaplains to minister to the coolies." I hope to meet the Committee of the Tamil Cooly Mission, and to submit to them my views upon the subject.

'Our correspondence upon these matters may now cease for the present.

'Believe me, your faithful servant in Christ,
(Signed) 'R. S. COLOMBO.'

And here the Bishop intended the matter to rest, at least for a time. He felt that the interchange of letters between himself and Mr. Oakley was not really an interchange of explanations, simply intended, and of a nature, to bring about mutual understanding. He had, indeed, wished his own letters to be such: but, from whatever cause, he felt that the correspondence, as a whole, had drifted into another manner, and was in danger rather of embittering feelings than of softening differences. And therefore he was resolved not to go on with it. Mr. Oakley did not, indeed, take the Bishop's desire to this effect quite literally, but sent one little rejoinder, written as follows:—

'NUWARA ELIYA, *June* 19, 1876.
'My Lord,—

'I have the honor to acknowledge, with my best thanks, receipt of your Lordship's letter of the 13th inst. As your Lordship has expressed a wish that the correspondence should cease for the present, I will only take the liberty of requesting your Lordship's attention to one point, on which I think there is still some discrepancy.

'It is possible that I have misunderstood your Lordship's meaning. If so I shall be glad to be corrected. Your Lordship admits that we are "at liberty, as formerly, to visit and instruct our people without let or hindrance from any of the Clergy of the island;"—but you add "It is my wish that the 'Missionary' should enter no 'Chaplain's' district without his knowledge; should he protest against their entrance I should as a rule require him to acquiesce. But should I find that the 'Missionary' was actually hindering his work, I should request the 'Missionary' not to enter that district." I regret to say that I cannot quite understand how it can be said that we are at liberty to visit, etc.—if we are only at liberty to enter a Chaplain's district with his consent, and if we are likely to be excluded from that district altogether, if our teaching is supposed to hinder the work of the Chaplain. I think your Lordship will perceive that there is a difficulty here which requires a little explanation.

'With much respect, I have the honor to be,' etc.,

(Signed) 'W. OAKLEY.'

This letter the Bishop did not answer. He had felt persuaded that the correspondence was not profitable: he had desired that it should cease. This desire he had meant to be taken literally; and when he found that he was nevertheless invited to enter into fresh definitions, he was not at all disposed to let himself be thus drawn into prolonging what he felt to be at once a wearisome and a profitless correspondence. I have sometimes found that his friends in England, reading the correspondence afterwards, in a historical manner, letter by letter, have wondered that he should have consented to let it end in this manner, with Mr. Oakley's unanswered question.

They may, probably enough, be right. I can only say that we, who were with the Bishop at the time, felt no such surprise. I do not think we ever thought of his answering it. I am afraid indeed that we were unreasonable enough to think both that it was not well that Mr. Oakley should have written it at all, and also that the inconsistency which he fastened upon was more apparent than real, verbally perhaps perplexing, yet involving no perplexity in practice; and therefore one whose solution it was needless to point out, inasmuch as it would present itself to those who were really eager to recognise it. I am prepared to be quite serious when I plead guilty, for my part, to having been mistaken in this, and in thinking that the Bishop's silence carried its own explanation; but for the present I am speaking history. Meanwhile, in proof of this seriousness, I will proceed to explain what I conceive the explanation and answer to be.

The stipulation then of the Bishop's, 'enter no Chaplain's district without his knowledge,' seems to me to mean, when translated into practice, 'make acquaintance with, and try to be on terms with, the Chaplains.' I never understood it to mean that before every individual service in each successive estate, the Missionary must make application to the Chaplain, and wait for his reply: but simply that if he found himself destined to range over the Chaplaincies of Messrs. A. B. C. and D, he should make a point of not ignoring them, but should put himself in communication, in the first instance, with Messrs. A. B. C. and D: should take care that they knew who he was, and what the nature of his commission and his work, in order that he might not be a stranger scheming across their schemes, unknown to them and ignoring them, found suddenly to their surprise holding examinations or services close beside them, but that each might at least understand, might expect and might respect each other's operations ; and, if possible, that each might co-operate with the other. Then lest it should chance that Mr. C. or Mr. D. should be a crotchetty person, disliking the Missionary's work, and wanting to exclude him, the Bishop explains that he on his part is prepared to insist that both Mr. C. and Mr. D. shall nevertheless recognise and accept the Missionary's freedom. Warm co-operation may indeed be impossible if they be morose : (this it is hoped will be attained with Mr. A. and Mr. B. ;) but the Bishop guarantees that all the moroseness of Messrs. C. and D, though it may limit their own usefulness and deprive the Missionary of the support they might have given him, yet shall not succeed in curtailing the Missionary's freedom. Surely this is his meaning. But then there is another alternative possible, and if the Bishop has once been driven into defining, how can he omit it? It may surely be that there may be no fault on the Chaplain's side, yet that the Missionary, through this prejudice or that, might be found to be really resisting and counterworking the Chaplain's blameless work. Is not this a possible alternative? and is it not one, which if you define at all, you must needs take account of? In this case, then, the Chaplain's appeal against the Missionary will not be disregarded : here is the one exception to the Bishop's 'rule' to insist on the Missionary's freedom in spite of the Chaplain ;—'should I find that he was actually hindering the work of the Chaplain, I should request the Missionary not to enter that district.' I cannot see how it was possible for the Bishop not to reserve to himself the right (as it would anyhow have been his duty) to interfere in such a case. But 'such a case' he instantly adds, 'as I understand it, is improbable in the extreme.' Is there any real inconsistency here at all? The Bishop no doubt promises freedom; but no freedom is, in the extremest sense, unlimited; nor is freedom necessarily contradicted by limitations; are then these particular limitations any contradiction to the freedom? The Missionary must not enter upon a Chaplain's district 'without his knowledge.' He must communicate with him; he must try to make friends with him, and if possible to come to understanding with him:—does this limit his own freedom? He is not bound to succeed in making friends; nor bound to relinquish the district unless he makes friends; on the contrary, if the Chaplain is impracticable the Bishop pledges himself to overrule the Chaplain: only on the one hypothesis, that the Missionary is doing definite harm, the Bishop reserves to himself the right of speaking and acting accordingly. Is this inconsistent with the promise of freedom to the Missionary? Mr. Oakley put forward two inconsistencies;—first that the freedom was contradicted by the need of obtaining the Chaplain's consent; but this in its apparent sense,—the sense which is fixed upon it by the use of the word 'consent,' the sense in which it really would subordinate the Missionary's liberty,—is not what the Bishop said: and secondly by the liability to exclusion from any district if his teaching was 'supposed to hinder' the work of the Chaplain. If 'supposed to hinder' means 'disliked by the Chaplain,' then neither is this reconcileable with what the Bishop had said; but if it means 'found after examination by the Bishop, to be in the Bishop's judgment an opposition-work,' then the *phrase* indeed is justifiable; but I am at a loss to see either how the Bishop could fail in such a case to interfere with the Missionary's action, or how anyone can reasonably characterize such hypothetical possibility of interference as a curtailment of liberty. I think it was thus that Mr. Oakley's rejoinder struck those who were with the Bishop at the time.

Thus then the correspondence ceases; and for awhile all seems to be silent. In passing from this, we pass from the stage of general tendencies or general attitudes, and come to an interchange of very definite actions. Before so passing, perhaps I may venture to say one thing which I strongly feel myself as to the Bishop's position during the months with which we have been dealing. I think, then, that we find the real key to the manner in which he thought, spoke, and acted, in a sentiment which he often expressed in one form or another, and which appears in letters to Mr. Oakley in such expressions as these, 'There is not in my plans, so far as I know them, anything that l may not trust the good sense and loyalty of the clergy to bring about as occasion requires.' Again, 'Such a collision I am sure need never occur. I am quite prepared to trust the good sense of both parties to avoid it.' That is to say, he desired a certain change. He desired that the Chaplains should begin to do Tamil work as well as the so-called Tamil Missionaries. He did not believe that the two agencies need be inconsistent if they were willing to be harmonious. He did not believe that he was asking for an adjustment in its own nature necessarily impossible, or even difficult. But he believed that the truest and simplest adjustment would be found in practice. Given that there were good sense and loyalty on both sides, he did not believe they really would fail to work into one another: and that there were these on both sides, he was bent on assuming. This was what he desired, and this was the mode by which he desired to reach it. He distinctly wished that both agencies might continue; but he wished them to supplement and work into each other. He did not desire to begin by defining accurately the limits of each. By degrees, it is true, he was driven into making statements which more and more came to have the character of definitions: but he did it only in the second instance, as he was compelled into it; he did it only by degrees, irregularly, and against his will; and he did it (if I may venture to think or say so) with less unassailable precision after all,—for the very reason that his own instinct went all in the contrary direction, of trusting to good sense, and loyalty, and mutual respect,—than it might have been done by one who had started with the taste for mathematically tabulated programmes, and limitations scrupulously defined.

My drift in making these remarks is of this nature. I believe that the definitions, as he gave them when pressed for them, sufficiently met the case; but

OF THE BISHOP'S POSITION.

I am not careful to prove that they met and covered it, with all its contingencies, in the most finished manner possible. If his own wish was rather not to define,—and he had defined once and again, not for definition's sake, but because challenged with the hypothesis of this or that which was presented as a difficulty: if moreover the precise detail of the difficulties themselves to be adjusted became familiar to him rather in the second instance than in the first; then it would neither be strange in itself, nor any fair reproach to him, far less any proof of indirect dealing or reservation of purpose, if what he said at an earlier time should seem to meet the precise point of hitch less precisely than what he was able to say at a later time,—if again that which he said at the later time, still seemed, if merely taken *ad pedem literae*, not wholly to have cut away all possibility of misconception. I do not say that his conversations and letters are fairly open even to this amount of criticism: but if anyone should think so, I am not careful to combat him; if they were ever so much so, I think that the fact would but bring into clearer light the true nature of his position. Given the one hypothesis which seemed to him self-evident, 'Chaplains ought to have *some* missionary work,' and first, middle, and last, his real position as to details was this—'there is not in my plans, so far as I know them, anything that I may not trust the good sense and loyalty of the Clergy to bring about as occasion requires.' First, middle, and last, his definitions, so far as he gave them, ought to be read by and with the light of this principle: and after all, when everything that was said on paper had been said, still it was to this principle that he looked—not only to supplement the written definitions, but to be (far more than the written definitions) the guide of conduct and the guarantee of successful adjustment;—there was nothing, he was convinced, which good sense and loyalty on the part of the Clergy would not of themselves, as occasion required, adjust harmoniously.

But to return to the events. At the date which we have now reached, the Bishop was away from Colombo, holding confirmations, etc. in the extreme south of the island. But within a fortnight or so of the ordination, there had begun to be one or two signs of further difficulties impending. They were all of the same kind, and all seemed to be indications of a definite, and what seemed to the Bishop a very dangerous policy, on the part of the directors of the Tamil Cooly Mission. What the nature of that policy was I may show by quoting words which will at all events not be open to any suspicion of adverse partisanship. They are taken from an account of the whole question drawn up by Mr. Jones on behalf of the Church Missionary Society, at the request of the Governor, which was reprinted from the 'Record' into the 'Guardian' of October the 18th:—

'There are in several parts of the island churches open to all denominations of Protestant Christians, and also some which are consecrated. These churches, the latter especially, are generally under the control of a Chaplain, who introduces, almost at will, whatever he may think desirable in the way of ornament, etc., and who also arranges hours of service. In places where Mission Churches have not yet been erected, the Missionaries have been in the habit of availing themselves of these for the native services, but generally without the idea of such an arrangement being permanent. It was both inconvenient and undesirable that the Mission congregations should be dependent on the arrangements of a Clergyman in no way connected with them. Occasionally too cases occurred where native Christians, who as converts from heathenism are very sensitive on the subject of idolatry, were offended at figures in painted windows, etc. which Europeans would not have objected to, and the introduction of crosses, etc. These reasons, taken in connection with the claims which would virtually have subjected those congregations to the Chaplain in whose church, though under another minister or catechist, they assembled, led the superintendent, Mr. Clark, to decide on removing his people from these churches to buildings which, as the property of the Mission, were under his control. Directions to this effect were given at three places, and the catechists assembled their congregations for service in Mission schoolrooms.'

The first instance I believe of this occurred at Kelebokka; of this place or of what happened there I know nothing beyond what I find in a Ceylon paper. The account however is I believe published with the knowledge of Mr. Clark himself. It is in these words:—

'Some time since the Tamil Christians of Kelebokka objected to attend divine service in the Church there, taking exception to figures in a chancel window. The same objection had previously been made in other places, and the heathen had in some instances taunted the Christians, saying that such images were entirely opposed to the catechist's denunciations of idolatry.

'Knowing these facts and being anxious to cherish in the minds of his people an abhorrence of anything which they considered idolatrous, Mr. Clark directed them to assemble for worship in a coffee store.'

The second instance was at Pusellawa. Here Mr. Auchmuty the newly-arrived Chaplain had, just at this moment, introduced a 'small wooden cross' upon the altar. His was one of the churches in which, besides his own services, there were habitually Tamil services conducted for the coolies. Either from the first, or at all events at the first mention of remonstrance from the Cooly Mission people (I do not know which), he withdrew the cross during the time of Tamil service, keeping it for his own English services only. Mr. Clark however remonstrated none the less, and was understood to threaten to withdraw the Cooly service from a church in which a cross was *ever* placed upon the altar, whether it were present during the Cooly services or no. When things were at this point, Mr. Auchmuty wrote to the Bishop. The Bishop wrote in reply advising Mr. Auchmuty to withdraw the cross altogether in deference to Mr. Clark's scruples; himself meanwhile undertaking to write to Mr. Clark, to guard against the withdrawal being taken as the concession of any principle of right or wrong in the matter, and in fact rather to protest (privately) against his conduct in requiring it. But before these things were accomplished, the Tamil congregation was finally withdrawn.

These two first instances were both I believe known to the Bishop, when a third and more important case of the same kind occurred. This was at Badulla. Now Badulla may be called (for the hill country) a considerable town.

It is in the centre of an important valley, encircled by considerable coffee plantations. But Badulla itself is by no means merely a coffee settlement. The coffee population would be English and Tamil, but Badulla has also a large Singhalese population, and was, I suppose, important in the Kandyan kingdom, before either English or coffee were introduced. Thus it happens that the Chaplain at Badulla, though like the others counted as a 'Bishop's' clergyman, is not himself English but Singhalese. He is indeed a thorough English scholar, as well as in other ways a vigorous and effective man; he takes the English services, and, as far as possible, English work among the planters round the district as well. He also knows some Tamil, and could, if need were, conduct a service in Tamil: (and just about this time he was studying Tamil further, which may very likely have been a cause of alarm:) but his own work primarily is pastoral and Mission work among his Singhalese countrymen. It is worth while to remember this: though for the present controversy he may be counted simply as a Chaplain.

In his church also there habitually was a Tamil service on Sunday afternoon, conducted not by him but by a Catechist of the Tamil Cooly Mission. He had not, indeed, any relations (I believe) with the Tamil congregation; and certainly when I was there in May, I thought him very shy of touching a Tamil, even in a case which might be thought to be one of emergency. But this church of his contained a painted window, and in the window was a figure. It is, I find, upon the fact of this painted figure that the withdrawal of the Tamil congregation from the church at Badulla is rested: or rather, I should say, upon the fact of the native Christians objecting to this figure. How far any such objection was really pressing I cannot of course say,—nor is it important when it appears from the authoritative Church Missionary Society's statement, that all these withdrawals were parts of a settled plan which was in large part independent of local difficulties: but I may mention for candour's sake, if it is thought worth while, that when I was myself in Badulla in May, one of the native Christians,—not Tamil but Singhalese, himself a most excellent man,—asked me (I quote from my journal) 'rather sorrowfully about the figure in the church's east window—were such things ordinary in England? He thought it hampered heathens in the understanding that Christians didn't kneel to worship an image.' However here, as in the former places, the order was given to withdraw from the church—and the Catechist withdrew his congregation to the schoolroom, together with the Tamil prayer-books, and if there be any such other little things as would represent the permanent settlement of the congregation.

But here came in a new fact. The congregation itself remonstrated. How far this was spontaneous on their part I cannot say. It is said that it was prompted by the English Government Administrator in the place: and this, in some manner or other, is possible enough. At all events they held a meeting — the Tamil congregation — in the church, under the Presidency of the Government Administrator. At this meeting they passed formal resolutions, deprecating, I believe, the withdrawal; but the precise form of the resolutions I have never heard; and these resolutions they forwarded to the Bishop.

The Bishop, when he received this appeal, took action at once. He wrote three letters. One he wrote to the Catechist in these words [1] :—

'Matara, *June* 30, 1876.

'Dear Sir,—

'Understanding that much regret has been felt at the discontinuance of the Tamil service usually held in S. Mark's Church, Badulla, at 2 p.m. on Sunday, I write to desire that at least until the matter shall have been fully enquired into, the service may if possible be resumed; and to forbid your holding any service on Sunday unless it be either the usual 2 p.m. service in church, or an additional service at some other hour.

'I remain your faithful servant in Christ,

(Signed) 'R. S. Colombo.

'To the Church of England Tamil Catechist,
Badulla.'

Another he wrote to the congregation, telling them, in similar manner, that, except on condition of the resumption first of the old service in church, he withdrew his sanction from any Tamil services conducted elsewhere; and a third

---

[1] It is necessary to mention that I have been obliged to copy this letter, and most of those that follow, from a sheet of the 'Examiner,' of Colombo. I am therefore rather at the mercy of misprints. Three or four of the more flagrant ones I am able to correct by my own knowledge of the original letters; though in correcting (as is sometimes necessary) a whole clause at a time, I cannot answer for the verbal accuracy of my recollection. For the rest, I can but copy what I find; but I do so with a painful consciousness of the extent to which misprints are possible, and I am bound to warn others also of the possibility of inaccuracies from this cause.

he wrote to the head of the Tamil Cooly Mission, Mr. Clark.

So quickly had these last events followed one another, that what the Bishop now wrote to Mr. Clark on this head is in the same letter which he had promised to write in respect of Mr. Auchmuty, and of the entire removal of his cross from the altar at Pusellawa. That former question seemed to be but secondary now. This secession at Badulla, if taken in connection with the two earlier cases, if it came really from Mr. Clark's order, seemed to show that he had adopted a line which was serious indeed. Though the consecrated church in which they had been accustomed to hold their services remained in the place and open to them as before, yet the Tamil congregation was henceforth to meet elsewhere; and this step was taken, first, without any communication with the Bishop; secondly, without any cause in itself pressing; thirdly, with an apparent pointedness of design which (however much it may said to be unintended) would certainly in fact be understood to mean separation from and condemnation of the churches, and the Chaplains, and their ways; or, with one degree of interpretation further, purgation from the distinctively 'Bishop's' clergy, with the Bishop whose representatives they were held to be, and their ways, and his ways. It seemed as if this were being done, and to be done, as a general plan over the coffee districts. It seemed, that is to say, as if, so far as the teachers of the Tamils could effect it, and so far as phrases so large are applicable to so small a development of Christianity, the 'Tamil Church' was henceforth to be a separated thing from the 'English Church in the coffee districts,' separated, in fact, from its organization; separated, in principle and in purity, from its superstitious practices. And it must not be forgotten how unreservedly such a separation would seem to endorse whatever uneasy suspicions the native converts might feel, as to the real idolatrousness of crosses or of painted windows. What the significance of the separation amounted to was in fact this: not the removal of all such things from the Church into which the converts had been baptized (for this was beyond the competency of the Tamil Mission); not an attempt to explain their meaning to the converts and reassure them against the fear of idolatry; but a confirmation of their worst fears; an acknowledgment that the ornaments *were* idolatrous; a proclamation therefore that the Chaplains and their congregations practised what was rightly stigmatized as idolatry; and a consequent open, unmistakeable act of separating from a part of the Church which had apostatized from pure worship, on the ground of its apostacy.

I am not pretending to say how much of this Mr. Clark meant, or did not mean; but I wish to show what seemed to the Bishop to be the real drift and nature of what Mr. Clark was doing, supposing (what it was difficult to doubt) that all these three secessions were ordered by him, and were parts of a single plan. It is to be remembered that some time before this, the Bishop had felt the Tamil Cooly Mission work to be at once inadequate in its extent, and open in its working to the suspicion of undue influence from those who owned no allegiance to the Church of England: that he had striven to supplement it by enlisting the Chaplains' energies for the same work; that his efforts had been consistently met by opposition; and now this opposition seemed to be taking the extreme and dangerous form of an organized standing apart from even the old outward show of partnership.

Will any one maintain that the Bishop, with these dangers before him, could have sat still or wholly held his hand? Remember again how in this last instance it was the congregation's own protest which challenged him. He felt, I cannot doubt, absolutely compelled, both as the ultimate protector of this congregation, and also as charged with the oversight of the whole flock of Christ's Church in Ceylon, and therefore as bound to maintain the Unity of the Body of Christ committed to him, to interpose and to prevent a policy whose true nature and issue seemed to him to be schism. The first immediate necessity he had tried to meet by his notes giving directions,• for the moment, to the catechist and the congregation. His third letter, was as follows :—

'MATARA, *June* 30, 1876.

'Dear Mr. Clark,—

'Mr. Auchmuty has shown me a letter from you, in which you request him to withdraw a cross which is placed upon the altar at Pusellawa church; I have recommended him to do so, since the utmost consideration is due from one clergyman for the scruples of another, who conducts services in the same church. At the same time I have undertaken to assure you that the concession involves no admission, as to the propriety or otherwise of such use of the cross, nor any pledge that it will not at any future time be replaced. To you I must say that

I consider your request unreasonable in itself, and an unwarrantable intrusion on the liberty of a brother clergyman. But to pass to a much more serious matter. I have received a copy of the minutes of the meeting of the Tamil congregation of S. Mark's Church, Badulla, held on the 18th of June ultimo, from which I learn that the Tamil service usually held in S. Mark's Church at 2 p.m. has been discontinued for some weeks, and that the catechist has been holding a meeting in the schoolroom at that hour.

'I trust that this may have occurred by no order of yours, but I write to you as head of the Tamil Cooly Mission, to beg that you will explain, if possible, an act which appears seriously to endanger the unity of the Church. Pending such explanation, I have written to the catechist to forbid his holding any service on the Sunday, unless it is either the usual 2 p.m. service in church, or an additional service at some other hour. I have also written to Mr. Alexander Bailey, the Tamil Churchwarden, to inform him that so long as the 2 p.m. service is discontinued, no other Tamil service in Badulla has my approbation. Earnestly praying that you may be able by an immediate answer to allay the anxieties which this change has created,

'I remain your faithful servant in Christ,
(Signed)   'R. S. Colombo.'

At this point we ought to turn to Mr. Clark. Now hitherto I have tried, as far as I could, not only to reproduce things said or written on one side or another, but to explain also something of the meaning and feelings of the actors. But in respect to Mr. Clark, from this point, I must not venture to offer myself as interpreter;

because, in truth, I know that I cannot interpret. His letters will speak for themselves, as far as they go; of the meaning from which they sprang, Mr. Jones' document, already quoted, will give us a little; I fear I cannot add more. To the Bishop's letter he wrote for the moment this reply:—

'KANDY, *July* 3, 1876.

'My Lord,—

'I beg to acknowledge the receipt of your letter of June 30th, which has just come to hand. I trust your Lordship will excuse the delay of a few days in replying to it. It refers to some matters of which I am at present in ignorance, and respecting which it will be needful for me first to make enquiry. I will write as soon as I can.

(Signed) 'WILLIAM CLARK.'

One other result of this delay of a few days is indicated in Mr. Jones' document, from which I learnt it for the first time, and (I confess) with some surprise. It is that before replying to the Bishop's appeal, Mr. Clark combined counsels with the rest of the body of Church Missionary Clergy. We take up Mr. Jones' statement exactly at the point at which our former quotation ended: 'On receiving intelligence of what had been done, the Bishop wrote direct to one of the Catechists, countermanding the orders he had received from the Superintendent, and directing him to resume the service in the church,—and then wrote to Mr. Clark, calling on him to clear himself from the charge of acting so as to cause schism.

'The Missionaries were at this time, early in July, assembled for their half-yearly conference, and Mr. Clark had thus an opportunity of obtaining the opinions of most of his fellow labourers.' It seems therefore that the attitude of feeling which requires to be expounded at this moment, and which Mr. Clark's subsequent letter must be taken to represent, is the attitude not (as I had been accustomed to suppose) of Mr. Clark alone, but of all. At all events, for that reason, Mr. Jones will be the surer exponent of it. He goes on: 'It was felt that as the catechists were the agents of the Society in London, neither could the Bishop claim, nor the Missionaries grant, absolute authority over them without the sanction of the parent Committee first obtained; and further, that the Bishop's action in countermanding the Missionary's orders to his own subordinate, without previous reference to him, was arbitrary and without precedent.' This is all that is given in description of the feeling of the conference.

Now if I profess inability to understand this feeling, it is not that I think the point here put forward unintelligible in itself;—far from it. Right or wrong, valuable or dangerous,—the point is obviously a real point; it is certainly intelligible, it certainly has some weight. But what *is* to me unintelligible is the general attitude to which this particular contention could present itself as a pertinent answer to the Bishop's letter. 'The Bishop,' Mr. Jones says, 'wrote to Mr. Clark, calling on him to clear himself from the charge of acting so as to cause schism. Is such a call, solemnly addressed to a clergyman by his Diocesan, an irrelevancy not needing to be taken account of in his reply? Granting that the Bishop may have acted unwisely,— granting that he may have acted, in Mr. Jones' own words, 'arbitrarily and without precedent' in sending his orders to the Catechist direct;—what is that to the grave presumption against Mr. Clark? To the Bishop, indeed, it had rather seemed that the presumption against Mr. Clark might be reason for his speaking at once to the Catechist, even if it were the unusual course; and I hardly know whether this thought will seem the less reasonable from the manner of Mr. Clark's reply;—but how can Mr. Clark's own position be altered, or the presumption against him affected one way or the other, by the Bishop's speaking meanwhile, be it ever so unusually, to the Catechist? and yet surely Mr. Jones' description of the real meaning of the Bishop's letter is exactly the right one.

But see how his statement goes on, proceeding to show in what way the feeling of the conference was translated into Mr. Clark's reply to the Bishop's letter. 'Mr. Clark, therefore, after consultation with his brethren, wrote to the Bishop to the effect that most reluctantly, and with all respect for his Lordship's office, he had been obliged to direct the Catechist to carry out the directions he had previously given, and at the same time he wrote through Mr. Cavalier to the Catechist giving him those instructions.' This is all his account of the answer. Indeed, whatever difficulty Mr. Jones may have had in describing the feeling of the conference in words which might seem to make it adequate to the occasion, whatever he may have felt himself of the inadequacy of the letter, as a reply to the question asked; in describing it he is as exact, and as direct, as in describing the Bishop's letter to which it replied. Here is the letter: it is long, but it is desirable to give it in full:—

'My Lord,— 'KOTTA, COLOMBO, *July* 7, 1876.

'I have now the honor of replying to your Lordship's letter of June 30th.

'With reference to the removal of the cross from the communion table in Pusellawa church, I beg to inform your Lordship that I made no request that it should be removed. Mr. Auchmuty himself wrote to me and voluntarily offered to remove it at the time of Tamil service. My letter was a reply to his, and was to the effect that as the placing of a cross on the table was illegal, I could not consent to the compromise he proposed. I think your Lordship will agree that there is nothing " unreasonable " in this, nor any "unwarrantable interference with the liberty of a brother clergyman."

'With regard to Badulla, I would very respectfully call your attention to the following particulars. The Tamil congregation of S. Mark's, so called, had no existence till June 18th, and has not therefore been in existence a single month. This so called congregation, as I learn from the Catechist, consists partly of Christians connected with the congregation, which till then held service in the school-room, and partly of *heathen*, who do not even express a wish to be Christians. It was formed, I am told, under the following circumstances. Mr. Sharpe, the Government Agent, issued a notice through Mr. Bailey, one of the Kachcheri writers, and a member of the Mission congregation, to the native Christians connected with the Mission, inviting them to meet at 2 p.m. in the church. They did so. A short service was held by the above Mr. Bailey, and a meeting was held at which Mr. Sharpe presided. Mr. Bailey was appointed churchwarden, and resolutions were passed, deciding that services should be held in the church, etc. These resolutions were subsequently transmitted to your Lordship as the voice of the Tamil congregation connected with S. Mark's, Badulla. I think I need not tell your Lordship that such a meeting was not a lawful church assembly. It was not assembled by notice from the minister as the law requires, nor with his knowledge, nor even with the knowledge of the resident catechist. It was a private meeting got up by one who was not even a member of the congregation. Such a meeting was to all intents and purposes illegal, and its proceedings null and void. But while repudiating the action of this meeting, and declining to adapt the conduct of the Mission to its resolutions, I must also respectfully ask your Lordship's permission to call your attention to one or two other particulars of great moment contained in your letter.

'You have prohibited the holding of divine service in the schoolroom, except as an additional service, and have required us to hold service in the church. This action involves a claim which has never been made by any of your Lordship's predecessors, either in India or Ceylon, a claim which would place Missionaries in a position which they have never hitherto occupied. The sphere of a Missionary is in all respects independent of that of a Chaplain, though occupying the same area, and therefore confers on the Missionary the right of freedom of action in his own work, whether as to time, place, or anything else. He is at liberty to hold services wherever and whenever he and his converts may please. He has always been acknowledged to possess that right, and has always exercised it. But if he were now to be *required* to hold service in a church, he would not only be deprived of this liberty, but would also practically be subordinate to the Chaplains. The church (except of course where it is the property of the Church Missionary

Society) is confessedly under the authority of the Chaplain and Trustees. The Missionary would therefore have to consult their will and wishes, as to when and where he should hold service. It would be in their power to restrain him from holding services in any place but their church. I need not say that this is a position into which the Missionaries will not suffer themselves to be drawn.

'Again, your Lordship has, without communication with Mr. Cavalier or myself, written to a Catechist of the Mission forbidding him to continue his services in the schoolroom. This too is altogether without precedent. Bishop Chapman did indeed at one time claim to give licenses to Catechists, but that claim was disallowed. But your Lordship has gone a long way beyond him in actually prohibiting the Catechist from holding service. The claim which this action necessarily involves will, I am sure, be regretted. Neither the Church Missionary Society, nor the Committee of the Tamil Cooly Mission, will consent to place its Catechists under the direct control of your Lordship. Catechists are lay agents of a lay society, and are directly responsible to the society only. The Bishop, as such, has authority over them only indirectly through the Missionary, and can no more claim a right to suspend their action, than a Bishop in England can suspend or restrain the action of a parish schoolmaster, or a scripture-reader.

'Under these circumstances I feel it to be my duty, a duty which I fulfil most reluctantly, and with all respect for your Lordship's office, to protest against your action in this matter, in the name of the Committee of the Tamil Cooly Mission, and to inform your Lordship that I have requested Mr. Cavalier to give instructions to the Catechist to go on with his work as before.

'I have the honour, etc., etc.,
(Signed) 'W. CLARK.'

I do not wish to dwell upon this letter; but it is necessary to observe in what way the Bishop is answered. Omitting the Pusellawa topic, which is now irrelevant, and the question whether the Badulla meeting in church was in any way formal or regular, upon which very little turns, the paragraphs which more immediately approach the subject are two. Mr. Clark had been called upon 'to clear himself from the charge of acting so as to cause schism.' He first protests indignantly against the liberty taken by the Bishop, in having anything to say to the Missionaries' conduct of services or disposal of their congregations; he secondly protests still more practically against the Bishop's venturing to attempt to restrain or touch the proceedings of a Mission Catechist (though the Catechist was for all intents and purposes the local minister of a regular congregation), and carries his protest into very overt action by formally announcing in conclusion that he has requested his subordinate to order the Catechist to disobey the written direction of the Bishop.

I need not enter further into the Bishop's feeling upon the matter. On receiving Mr. Clark's letter he at once wrote a little note to Mr. Cavalier (who, like the other Church Missionary Society's clergy, was already at Kotta, and therefore within easy reach of Colombo) thus:—

'COLOMBO, *July* 8, 1876.
'Dear Mr. Cavalier,—

'Matters of great importance make it desirable that I should see you as soon as possible. I hope you will make it convenient to call upon me here before 1 p.m. on Monday next the 10th.

'In the meantime let me earnestly beg you, for your own sake, to take no further steps in reference to the Church at Badulla.

'I remain
'Your faithful servant in Christ,
(Signed)   'R. S. COLOMBO.'

Meanwhile on the day which intervened between this note and Mr. Cavalier's visit (Sunday, July 9), the Bishop wrote again to Mr. Clark.

'COLOMBO, *July* 9, 1876.

'Dear Mr. Clark,—

'With the greatest pain I have to reply to your letter of the 7th instant. I write with a deep sense of the responsibility which is laid upon me; and as I have prayed earnestly for the Holy Spirit's guidance in the writing of this letter, so I have entreated Him to guide you to receive it rightly. As to the congregation at Pusellawa, I understood your letter to Mr. Auchmuty to mean that unless the cross were altogether removed, you would remove the Tamil congregation altogether from the church. "I know," you say, "this is what you would like to avoid." I trusted that you also had wished to avoid so grave a step, and had therefore written what you did in order to obtain the other alternative, the removal of the cross. When you spoke of the placing of the cross on the communion table obliging you to an act which no Churchman could think of without pain, I understood you to be requiring the removal of the cross. But you tell me you made no such request. I must therefore infer that you proceeded, without first trying every other course, without consulting your Bishop, "to remove the Tamil congregation altogether from the church." I fear you do not see the wrongfulness of this act, but it amounts to causing division in the church.

It is the encouragement of separation, the formation of a separate congregation which, though living near the consecrated church, and prevented by no external cause from using it, should yet meet elsewhere for worship. Such an act cannot be tolerated in the Church of God, and if persisted in must involve sad consequences. It is from the charge of encouraging a similar act at Badulla that I desired you to clear yourself in my letter of the 30th instant.

'From that charge you are not at present cleared. In your letter of the 7th inst. you scarcely deal with it at all, but tell me there was no congregation of S. Mark's, Badulla, till the 18th ultimo, a statement which I cannot understand. There certainly was one a few months ago, when I myself ministered to it, and I am informed that it continued to meet for service in the church until a few weeks ago. The legality or illegality of the meeting of June 12th is not in question. I referred to its resolutions simply as evidence of a fact which you do not appear to deny, viz. that either you or Mr. Cavalier encouraged an act of separation, similar to that which you yourself seem to have originated at Pusellawa. In the third part of your letter, where you state that "the Missionary is at liberty to hold services wherever and whenever he and his converts may please," you are in grievous error. On the contrary he holds such services only by, and during, the consent of the Bishop, which consent may be at any time withheld or withdrawn at the Bishop's absolute discretion. Now you have, as stated in your letter, encouraged at Badulla (by requesting Mr. Cavalier to give such instructions to the Catechist) a service which I expressly told you, in my letter of the 30th inst., "has not my approbation." Further this was a service I had expressly forbidden, in the exercise of my lawful authority. For observe,—the Catechist, if not a mere brawler, is a person exercising an office in the Church; he is therefore subject to the Bishop's authority. All services held in the Church of God are held under the sanction and with the authority of the Bishop. All lay people who are faithful to the Church will keep away from services of which the Bishop has written to them that they have not his approval; yet you have encouraged a Catechist to disobey the written direction of the Bishop; you have desired services to be held which the Bishop has directly forbidden, and have encouraged the lay people to attend them. The offence of causing division at Pusellawa and Badulla, or either of them, must, if proved against you, be treated as extremely serious. The other offence of promoting disobedience is almost equally grave. I still entertain a hope that you may be able to furnish some explanation of the facts which may place your conduct in a different light. I therefore solemnly desire you, either to furnish such an explanation, or to undo the fault you have committed, first by desiring the Tamil Christians at Pusellawa to return to the church for service at the usual hour; secondly, requesting Mr. Cavalier to give similar directions at Badulla; thirdly, by writing yourself to the Catechist at Badulla to urge him to obey and not to disobey my letter. I shall accept your own written assurance as evidence that this admonition has been complied with, and will grant you a week in which to execute it, heartily praying that God of His great goodness will give you grace to do His will.

'Unless either the explanation or the assurance just spoken of reaches me before Tuesday the 18th inst., I shall consider my admonition to have been contumaciously disregarded.

'Believe me your faithful servant in Christ,
(Signed)   'R. S. Colombo.'

'P. S. Although the Catechists are—as holding an office in the Church—subject to the Bishop, yet I should be very reluctant to insist on or use that authority, but should, as a rule, deal with them through the ordained Clergyman; but the case being an exceptional one, in which the Clergyman was himself under grave suspicion with reference to the matter treated of, I had recourse to the power which I undoubtedly possess of direct interference, reporting to you at the same time the steps which I was taking. R. S. C.'

On the next day after the writing of this letter, Mr. Cavalier came, according to the Bishop's desire, to call upon him. The Bishop had wished to show him what would be the true nature of compliance with the directions of Mr. Clark, and to urge him to think well before complying; but Mr. Cavalier said that it was already too late, for he had written and sent his letter to the Catechist. The Bishop, greatly concerned, tried still to show him something of what such action meant, and asked how he could have been induced to write the letter. Mr. Cavalier replied that it was done by the advice of the Church Missionary Clergy assembled for conference at Kotta.

This conversation took place on Monday, July 10th. Now it happened that the Bishop was bound by an engagement made, I believe, some time before any of these last complications had begun, and certainly irrespective of them all, to call upon the Clergy at Kotta, and have some conversation with them, the very next morning after this, Tuesday, July 11th. To this conversation he had looked, he says, (speaking with reference to his former correspondence with Mr. Oakley,) 'finally to set at rest the remaining apprehensions.' But, as we have seen, during the ten days before his appointed time of interview there had arisen—not indeed (so far as his knowledge went) with the Church Missionary Society, but with Mr. Clark personally and his conduct of the special Cooly Mission—a question more serious than any of the former. And finally, on this last day, at the very moment (as it were) before his long arranged conversation with the Church Missionary Society's Clergy, he is confronted suddenly with the consternating announcement, that not only has Mr. Cavalier fully thrown in his lot with Mr. Clark, but moreover the assembled body of Church Missionary Clergy has taken upon itself, and identified itself with, the whole policy and conduct of Messrs. Clark and Cavalier. The occasion was difficult indeed, and formidable. The Bishop could but pray for wisdom and truth of heart for himself and them, and trust the issue to GOD. Meanwhile he never shrank from going straight forward. He kept the old engagement, and went next morning to Kotta. But before entering upon other points he felt bound, he said, to ask whether it was really true, as he had yesterday been given to understand, that they had combined to urge Messrs. Clark and Cavalier, when desired by the Bishop to explain acts which seemed schismatical, to meet him in reply with protest and formally avowed disobedience. They did not answer at once, but when they answered, their answer was that this thing 'though not a Resolution of the Conference as such, had been discussed in the Conference, and was done by their unanimous advice.' I quote a phrase of the Bishop's, in which he shortly afterwards described what happened at this time. Parallel to this is the account published at the time in the Colombo papers,—necessarily by some one of the Clergy present,—of 'Notes of conversation held with the Bishop of Colombo, Tuesday, July 11th, 1876.' We find there, 'It was replied that although the letter did not proceed from the Conference, the action taken had been fully discussed and approved.' I feel bound to quote these two statements in particular reference to the fact emphasized in Mr. Jones' paper, and which was new to me when I read it there, that 'of the Clergymen present, two at least had not been called on to express any opinion on the question. One had joined the Conference only that morning, and had only a general knowledge of what had occurred.' It is greatly to be regretted for every one's sake, that if any distinction could be drawn at all between the positions in which the several Clergy stood, the Bishop should have been given to understand that there was none.

Now there are two points, both indeed clearly contained in the account I have given, upon which I desire somewhat more definitely to concentrate attention, because I think that much of the first impression and offhand judgment respecting the Bishop's action turns upon misconception with regard to them. The first is, that the particular point of fatal divergence between him and Messrs. Clark and Cavalier, was in no respect of his seeking, or of his making. He declared no war. He began no aggression. He never, as some have supposed, came down with an unnecessary statement of Episcopal claims, and suspended all who declined to subscribe to it. But *they* initiated a policy, which seemed to be a policy of separation. The

Bishop comes in merely as defending the congregation, on the congregation's own appeal, from enforced separation. They decline to explain; they protest against his interference; and specially, leaving or trying to leave all other issues, fasten upon the one particular act of his which implied the hypothesis that all congregations of the Church and their accepted ministers (not only if fully commissioned, but through whatever necessity accepted as ministers) were integral parts of that One Sacred Body, whereof he was by a divine commission, which he dared not undervalue, the appointed Chief Pastor: upon this act they fasten, and from henceforth the main quarrel is made to turn upon this hypothesis, and their protest against it. But we will not go off upon this question now: for with Messrs. Clark and Cavalier at least the real quarrel did *not* rest on this. I wish it to be clearly kept in view that their action first, and secondly their mode of resenting his interference and replying to his demand for explanation, left him absolutely no choice whatever but to act. Whether suspension of the licenses was or was not the only available mode of action I do not say: but I do say that action, clear and brave, in defence of individual congregations, in defence of the Unity of the Church, in vindication of insulted authority, had suddenly become, through no act nor choice of his own, through no circumstances of his own creating or seeking, inexorably and inevitably his bounden duty.

And the second point on which I desire to fix attention is this. It was assuredly by no act or wish of his, that when he found himself in this position, and before he had time to deal with the matter at all, or to speak a word, he suddenly found himself confronted not with two, but with twelve. Before he had time to speak or move, the assembled Church Missionaries had identified themselves with the Tamil Cooly Mission, and made its acts their own. A body of Clergy, one of whom, as all the world has been told if they have been told nothing else, was already at work in the island before he was born—(Mr. Jones' document enumerates their different terms of service with some emphasis of detail)—had thrust itself into the fatal position of Messrs. Clark and Cavalier. This, moreover, came to him quite suddenly, at the very last moment, and so ostentatiously that he could not pretend to ignore it. Well might we expect to hear that a Bishop, young almost without precedent, and of very little experience,—as again all the world knows him to be, though they know not a syllable about him besides,—would have shrunk from maintaining anything in the face of so perplexing an array of experience and authority. And he, I suppose, if he had been able to feel the smallest doubt as to the sacred truth and cogency of the principles which he was challenged to defend, might probably have shrunk. But he was not able either to doubt, or to shrink. Again I am not saying whether it was absolutely inevitable, even now, that he should extend to the ten, in conformity with their own most perplexing choice, that action which he felt compelled to take in respect of the two; whether it might not have been possible, even now, to separate the ten from the two, and in the face of the avowal of the ten that the act of the two was their act, still to deal only with the two directly, and with the ten only indirectly, through the two: or rather I do not mind going further, and avowing that I believe this course *was* possible, and that I much regret that it was not the course taken: but this I will say, that it was not the Bishop who put the ten into the dock beside the two,—they had thrust themselves in, and he to his consternation had found them there, professing their community with the two; it might have been possible for him still to insist upon their removal thence before passing sentence, but at least he had not intruded them into it, but themselves, and it would have required at least very resolute insistance on his part to have broken, by his own act, the bands of the partnership with which he was challenged.

Now at this moment the relation of the two sides to one another is, I think, sufficiently clear. They stand face to face upon a definite and a single issue. The issue has risen out of action within the Tamil Cooly Mission, but the action in question, with all that it involves, has been adopted by the Church Missionary Society as such. The immediate mode of the action (which is part of what has been adopted) seems, as regarded from the Bishop's point of view, to contain—first, a line of conduct perilously schismatical, at all events unless adequately explained; and secondly, a definite act of contumacious disobedience. But it may be that the conduct which looked schismatical was capable of some explanation: and at all events at the moment when this remained an open question, defiance was deliberately preferred to explanation on grounds of principle. It follows, therefore, that whatever be the inevitable consequences of this particular disobedience in respect of the individuals, the real question of universal interest throughout the Church will rather be the question as to the ground of principle upon which so unusual a course was justified. When then it is asked, what were the grounds of principle, we shall, I think, most conveniently answer that there were two. They are branches indeed of one; but we shall gain much in clearness by taking them separately.

First, and most obviously, there is the claim that Catechists and congregations under the Society are so entirely independent of Episcopal control, that if the Bishop makes any attempt to touch them, the Society's Clergy are justified in countermanding and overruling, openly in the face of the Catechists and congregations, that which the Bishop has directed. This statement contains two distinguishable thoughts: the first that the Catechists, etc. have a right to independence; and the second, that the Bishop's attempt to give them any directions is so definitely an outrage, as to justify ecclesiastical contumacy. I do not see that either part of this statement is really invalidated by the admission of which Mr. Jones' paper speaks, 'the Missionaries expressed regret that unintentional discourtesy had been shown to his Lordship, in not communicating with him previous to confirming the orders given to the Catechist,' for this implies no hesitation as to the propriety of the orders given, or of their confirmation after the preliminary courtesy of communicating with the Bishop, that is (I suppose) after giving him the opportunity of himself recanting an act, which, failing his recantation, the Missionaries would proceed to overrule. This then is one principle upon which the Missionaries base and subsequently defend their conduct. 'Catechists,' as Mr. Clark says, 'are lay agents of a lay society, and are directly responsible to that society only;' or, in the words of a resolution passed on July 14th, 'The authority claimed by the Bishop over Catechists, congregations, and places of worship we cannot yield for reasons already given.' I may just remind you by the way how very large a proportion of the whole Church organization it is (under such circumstances as those in Ceylon) on behalf of which this peremptory claim to extra-diocesan independence is set up: but I must not pause to say a word upon the question itself of the important principle here at issue. Very important it is, and very much there is that might be said on the subject: but I must be content to rest with pointing out, as fact, that here is the first great principle which is in question.

But it will be felt that this is not all. The conduct of the Missionaries which the Bishop wished to have explained was in itself entirely independent of the Bishop's subsequent letter to the Catechist. The contention just described was provoked by that letter of the Bishop's: it can hardly therefore stand by itself as the ground of the Missionaries' tacit refusal of explanations. This seems to rest upon a further principle, according to which not only the *lay* portion of the Church is exempt from all episcopal control, but also Missions, as Missions, in all their parts, not only in respect of the lay subordinates, but also in respect of the clerical directors, are outside of the domain of the Bishop's authority. 'The sphere of a Missionary is in all respects independent of that of a Chaplain, though occupying the same area, and therefore confers on the Missionary the right of freedom of action in his own work, whether as to time, place, or anything else. He is at liberty to hold services wherever and whenever he and his converts may please. He has always been acknowledged to possess that right, and has always exercised it. But if he were now to be *required* to hold service in a church, he would not only be deprived of this liberty, but would also practically be subordinate to the Chaplains.' At first sight Mr. Clark seems in these words to be protesting against the arbitrary interference of a Chaplain : but when it is remembered that the Chaplain at Badulla had not (so far as I have ever heard) stirred a finger or spoken a word,— that it was the Bishop and the Bishop only who had pretended to limit the otherwise unlimited liberty of the Missionary,—that therefore the protest in these words is necessarily against the Bishop's interference, and that it is as against Episcopal right that the strong statement of the Missionary's uncontrollable discretion is formulated; further still, that the sentences here quoted are the answer and the only answer which Mr. Clark returns to a solemn demand from the Bishop that he should explain an apparent excess of private liberty in his missionary management; it will be felt that, however little it may be stated in direct words, or recognizable upon the surface of the subsequent discussions,—(and I will willingly add, however little it may have been realised or intended by the Kotta conference itself)—there is underlying the action taken by Mr. Clark, and adopted by all the Church Missionaries together, a claim for the practical independence of any Mission, as a Mission, from the ultimate control of the Bishop.

Upon these two principles, then, the Missionaries defend, as necessary and proper, what the Bishop can only regard as conduct in itself dangerous to the Church, and culminating in direct contumacy. Here is the issue—intelligible, direct: its statement has been tedious, but its significance is clear.

As against these principles the Bishop sets forth the authority, inseparable from responsibility, involved in the commission which he has received from God as Chief Pastor of the Church of Christ in the Diocese of Colombo. The commission is one which he dare not treat as human; from the responsibility and authority which are inherent in it he dare not shrink. It is not that he desires to employ himself in meddling with the conduct of Missions, or assuming the direction of Society's Catechists; but having once so acted under circumstances of urgency which seemed to him to require such action, he finds his right so to act under any circumstances—the ultimate right, the right in the abstract, the principle of the right—defied and denied as matter of principle. He cannot tolerate the defiance without accepting the denial of the principle; he cannot, under the circumstances, accept the denial of the principle without incurring the guilt of undervaluing and impairing the sacred deposit of Episcopal responsibility, and its concomitant authority, solemnly committed to him by the commission and in the Name of God. He laid down to them the principles of this authority, as authority in the last resort, carefully pointing out how rarely and how reluctantly he thought that it should be exercised; but its existence they entirely denied. Of the principle really at issue he afterwards says: 'The matter is not one of a little less, or a little more, in the way of concession; it is not really a question whether the Bishop asks a little too much, or the Clergy refuse a little too peremptorily. The real issue appears to me to be touched by a question which

I put at Kotta: With whom does the ultimate responsibility for the souls of these people rest, with the Bishop or with the Church Missionary Committee in London? The answer I received was 'With the Committee.' My answer would have been, in the words of the Apostolic Canons (No. 39, quoted by Bingham, ii. 3. § 2), οἱ πρεσβύτεροι καὶ οἱ διάκονοι ἄνευ γνώμης τοῦ ἐπισκόπου μηδὲν ἐπιτελείτωσαν· αὐτὸς γάρ ἐστιν ὁ πεπιστευμένος τὸν λᾶον τοῦ Κυρίου, καὶ ὁ ὑπὲρ τῶν ψυχῶν αὐτῶν λόγον ἀπαιτηθησόμενος.

I believe we have now arrived exactly and truly at the point of the principle which is really at issue. It is not a question of the most convenient form of ordinary administration. It is a question of ultimate right in extreme cases. As a question, then—not of ordinary management, but of abstract right and ultimate responsibility—is a Society's Mission, or, if not this (for this, I suppose, will not be persistently maintained), yet is every part of the Mission, except the three or four ordained Clergy,—are the congregations,—are the Catechists, who are their ordinary Ministers,—are their Services,—independent of all Episcopal supervision and control: dependent, instead thereof, upon the ultimate control and jurisdiction of a private Society? If this question were met by a temperate but decided negative on the part of the Society, then I verily believe, for my own part, that whatever might remain of personal discomfort or perplexity of local circumstances, there would be no question of principle at issue in the Diocese of Colombo. I understand, of course, that the Society could not thus answer the question, without thereby declining to sustain their Ceylon representatives in a contrary answer, without further requiring that their representative who made the contrary answer a sufficient ground for open disobedience to the Bishop, should no less openly reverse his attitude: but I trust that the Society would not be overruled in its decision on an important question of principle by thoughts like these. As to the question itself, the negative answer to it seems, I confess, to me, in principle, though not in terms, to be almost if not altogether required by their own published statement of their principles of constitution and working. Even if I am altogether wrong in seeming to see any such thing implied already in their published documents, yet may it not be supposed that that great number of members of the Church of England, clerical and lay, who are the strength of the Church Missionary Society, will feel, as loyal sons of the Church, that the constitution of the Church inevitably involves it?

Note.—Since this was written, the Church Missionary Society in London has published resolutions in a very contrary spirit. I will not quote them, for I am persuaded that they cannot be permanent in their present form. But at all events, it would seem from them the more inevitable that the question of principle must be weighed and settled authoritatively on its own merits as a question of principle; inasmuch as it is the less likely that any preliminary concession, or compromise in the immediate case, will postpone the necessity of settlement.

But I am digressing. What I have said, and that only, I believe to be the question of principle at issue. And if, exactly in this position of affairs, and in the presence of this simple issue, the Bishop had forthwith proceeded to withdraw the licenses, there would have been, I believe, far clearer appreciation than there has been, both in England and (still more emphatically) in Ceylon, of the principles really in question. But before the moment of withdrawal another topic was introduced, in itself, no doubt, important enough, and yet, as I believe, altogether secondary to the universal importance of the question of principle. The introduction of this topic seems to me to have seriously complicated the understanding of the whole question in England, and almost totally (at least in the early days) to have banished any right understanding of it in Ceylon. In order to explain its introduction, I must go back and remind you of three or four things.

First, it must be remembered that, many weeks before, the Bishop had seen cause to be seriously discontented with the working of the Tamil Cooly Mission on two grounds: the one, that it was inadequate; the other, that its constitution, though not directly involving 'unsectarian' teaching, seemed by its indirect influence to give a very vague and nondescript character to great part of the Christianity taught.

It must be remembered, further, that these two grounds of dissatisfaction, taken in connection with the attempt of the 'Mission' to insist on monopoly of Cooly preaching, had caused the Bishop to feel, some weeks before this, that sooner or later the day must come when the Cooly work, either by transformation or by disallowing of the existing 'Mission,' would have to be organized anew upon a more satisfactory basis.

Further, it should be known, that the second of the two grounds of dissatisfaction mentioned above, had been considerably strengthened by the line of criticism publicly adopted against the Bishop's rumoured designs of aggression upon the Mission. The 'unsectarian' nature of the Mission and Committee were emphasized, as constituting a valid reason for the exemption of the Mission from any action of the Bishop. The same effect was produced by the manner in which Mr. Clark, one time and another, rested his unwillingness to treat with the Bishop about modifications in the Mission on the necessity of reference to the Committee. This culminated when, shortly before the time we are dealing with, the Bishop expressed his wish to meet the Committee and talk over the matter with them, and they declined to confer with him, inviting him instead, if he wished for any modification of the operations of the Mission, to lay his proposals before the Committee in writing.

Fourthly, it must be remembered that the second of the two principles, as I have ventured to draw them out above, which underlay Mr. Clark's letter of July 7th, seemed to amount to a peremptory claim for the complete independence of any constituted 'Mission' from Episcopal interference: and of course it is obvious also to point out that it was in reference to the Tamil Cooly Mission that the letter was written.

And, fifthly, the Bishop found himself face to face (as he considered) with the immediate necessity of suspending the licenses, and therefore disallowing the ministrations of both the two English Missionaries who formed the chief link of connection (and always, as the Bishop feared, a link of questionable sufficiency) between the Cooly Mission organization and the Church Missionary Society, and therefore the Church of England.

These considerations, taken together, will, I think, explain the Bishop's feeling, that if, on behalf of the Tamil Cooly Mission, under all existing circumstances, there were set up a claim to independence of the Bishop and the Diocese, then it was necessary that he should in reply to that, and at this time, constitute afresh the work of the Church of England among the coolies. If the Tamil Cooly Mission were an integral part of the Church, he would be within his right, while forced to suspend its present directors, in taking its direction under Diocesan control; if it were not so, and the claim for independence of the Diocese, that is, of Church organization, were persisted in upon the so-called 'unsectarian' principle, then it was time that the Church of England should cease to accept it as her substitute, and should organize some work among the coolies which would be her own. When, therefore, he had explained at Kotta the principles of his authority over the whole Church, not as for daily exercise, but as in the last resort inherent and inalienable, and they had denied that any such authority existed, he told them that unless this were conceded he could not allow the Tamil Cooly Mission to go on as before, but should take the work under his own direct management. He told them that before he could consent, after all that had been said and done, to continue to accept the work of the Mission as the Church of England's work among the coolies, two conditions were necessary: the first, that it should be, in its working, free from all control by the local mixed committee; the second, that the Bishop should have a veto on the appointment of Catechists, and ultimate authority over all congregations and services. These conditions they would not concede. The conversation then went back to the general question of principle, but without any good result: as they had at first recommended the course adopted by Messrs. Clark and Cavalier, so now they fully maintained it. There seemed to be no prospect of bridging the chasm. Then it was that the Bishop withdrew the licenses of them all, adding, at the same time, that this withdrawal would be cancelled in respect of all who, by the following Saturday, should acknowledge the principle of his claim.

THERE was therefore an interval of four days more before the suspension was fully ratified. It is right that I should give some account of what happened during these remaining days. There are two sets of things to be spoken of. On the one hand there are attempts—earnest but fruitless—to bring about a common understanding, or compromise, such as both sides might be able to accept, and so to avert even now the final catastrophe: and on the other hand there are steps taken by the Bishop for new arrangements of work among the Tamil coolies. These latter steps may perhaps be mentioned first; for they unfortunately had part in defeating the attempts at reconciliation. Those attempts must be described, too, for the sake of completeness and truth: yet though they may help to elucidate, they unhappily do not otherwise advance the matter. Yet one thing more they do, if I may venture without presumption to say it; they show, I believe, the 'spirit of meekness' in which matters were conducted. But first as to steps with regard to the Cooly Mission. On Wednesday, July 12th, the Bishop wrote two letters. One was a circular letter sent round to all subscribers to the Tamil Cooly Mission; it is as follows :—

'Colombo, *July* 12, 1876.

'Dear Sir,—

'I have thought it necessary to take a somewhat sudden step with regard to the Tamil Cooly Mission, of which you have been a supporter; and I feel it due to you that I should not lose a day in explaining to you what I have done and why.

'In my late tours in the coffee districts of the Central Province, I found that the results of the Mission were not thought entirely satisfactory. The schools were said sometimes to languish from want of efficient supervision; the visits of Catechists were thought too few and too brief, while the English Missionaries, however great their zeal and ability, could hardly make their presence felt throughout so large an area. I was myself convinced, so far as I could form an opinion in so short a time, that the success, especially in the matter of schools, had not been at all proportionate to the effort made; and that it would not be so, until the Mission were strengthened by enlisting the supervision of English clergy resident in each district.

'I have accordingly been for some time endeavouring to obtain a share in the work for the resident Chaplains, whose numbers I hope speedily to increase (two more will, I hope, be at their posts within a few weeks), but my efforts in this direction met with resolute opposition from the Superintendent of the Mission, who bitterly resented any intervention on the part of the Chaplains.

'Under these circumstances I have found it necessary—an interview with the Tamil Cooly Mission Committee having been denied me—to insist on the Superintendent's withdrawal, and to take this part of the work of the Church of England more directly under my own care. In order to prevent interruption of the work, I have thought it best to proceed with the utmost promptitude. The new system starts to-day, and I hope will take the place of the old without perceptible intermission. Nor will any visible change be obtruded upon you, unless it be more frequent visitation of your schools, and a larger number of clergy engaged in the work.

'The Archdeacon will henceforth be the centre and acting head of the Tamil as well as of the English work throughout the coffee districts; the Chaplains in each district, aided by native clergy and Catechists—their Tamil curates—will conduct and supervise it on the spot.

'It is with much regret that I have found myself compelled to proceed with a rapidity which may seem, at first sight, disrespectful to the supporters of the Tamil Cooly Mission; but I can assure them it is with sincere respect and gratitude to those who have assisted the cause so far that I have taken this step which was needed for its further prosperity.

'Having thus laid before you an outline of the nature and reasons of this change, I have only to express my earnest hope that you will continue to so useful and important a work all the sympathy and encouragement and pecuniary support which you have hitherto afforded.

'I am, dear Sir, yours very faithfully,
(Signed) 'R. S. COLOMBO.'

On the same day he wrote another to the members of the Tamil Cooly Mission Committee:—

'COLOMBO, *July* 12, 1876.
'Dear Sir,—

'For the better working of the Church of England's Mission to the Tamil Coolies, I have found it necessary to make very considerable alterations in the system under which it has hitherto been conducted. These alterations have involved, I regret to say, the withdrawal of the Rev. W. Clark from the superintendence of the work, and the transference of the whole to the direct care of the Bishop. The new system starts to-day, and the work will, I hope, go on without any perceptible check.

'I feel bound to apprise you of this change at this the earliest possible opportunity, and to assure you of my regret that I have been obliged to make it without a previous interview with the Committee. I asked for such an interview, but you may remember that it was considered undesirable.

'Let me express to you at the same time my gratitude to the Committee of the Tamil Cooly Mission, for the zealous aid which they have so long given to the Christian cause, and my sincere regret for any disappointment or annoyance which the sudden step I have been compelled to take may cause you.

'I trust that you will still continue to help the work of the Church among the Tamil coolies under the new conditions, and will allow your name to remain upon the list of the Committee.

'I remain, dear Sir, yours very faithfully,
(Signed) 'R. S. COLOMBO.'

Upon these letters it is necessary that I should remark that they are certainly misleading, in at least one important particular, as to the nature of the Bishop's proceedings. If I am told that this is an audacious comment, I cannot help it. I am not engaged, here or elsewhere, in defending the Bishop. My task is simply to explain, as far as possible, what his acts were, and what their meaning was, in order that English Churchmen may have, what hitherto they have not had, the means of judging the whole question for themselves. In the present instance I have shown what his acts were, by quoting the letters: but knowing as I do how much those who read these letters have been misled by them into mistakes as to the Bishop's meaning, it is necessary that I should add this fact also. The point is this: many of those who read these letters understood the Bishop to be attempting to appropriate to himself, by arbitrary compulsion, the whole existing organization of the Tamil Cooly Mission. They understood him to mean that he was seizing the schools and chapels and funds of the old Mission, as well as driving into a forced allegiance to himself those Catechists and schoolmasters whom the Mission had procured and trained in its own ways. And understanding this they looked forward to the certainty of the failure of the attempt; or if they found him afterwards in a different attitude, assumed that he had changed his ground through the ignominious force of failure. But in fact, whatever these letters may be thought to convey, he certainly never had contemplated such an idea as possessing himself of the property of other people. As he says a few days later, 'I did not disown it, because it had never occurred to me.' And the same thing applies to the idea of his forcing Catechists, etc., into allegiance to himself. He did indeed consider himself to be rearranging the authorized Church of England work among the coolies; and thought it, probably, possible enough that there might be many among them under those circumstances who would be glad to range themselves with his rearranged work; most of them would probably be attached to him if the Committee[1] mostly accepted his act; if few or none of the Committee remained with him, the Catechists might also, as a body, stand aloof: but certainly he never had thought of taking possession of them and their organization and their services compulsorily. And if the old machinery should *not* attach itself to him, then the meaning of his action was not so much that he 'assumed' to himself, or 'appropriated,' or 'took into his own hands' the old machinery: as that in that case he felt himself obliged to disown, to ignore, to set aside the old machinery, and to organize new modes of working in its stead. He would indeed 'take into his own hands;' but that which he would take, was not the old machinery for working (which was private property), but the field of work itself, in order to be sure that by new means the Church did that work effectively which she could no longer acknowledge to be adequately done on her behalf, as it was now being done by so much as remained in working order of the old machinery.

But in the necessity for this explanation there is (I think) illustration enough of the manner in which the action taken with regard to the Cooly Mission, and put before the public through the two quoted letters, was unfortunately calculated to impress the minds of people in Ceylon at the moment, and carrying them away upon the excitement of this collateral issue, to confuse them hope-

---

[1] It needs to be remembered that when the Committee is spoken of as 'unsectarian,' or as representing the 'unsectarian' principle; this merely means that amongst its members were representatives of various denominations,—it does not mean that there were not amongst them many members of the Church of England.

lessly as to the real principle, distinct in truth from this collateral issue, and far more important than it, yet by the course of events blended almost inextricably with it,— which was meanwhile so solemnly and so seriously in question at Kotta.

Upon this action taken by the Bishop in respect of the Cooly Mission there will be a few words to be added presently. At this moment we are dealing with a certain interval of four days, July 11th–15th, and must not pass beyond that limit without first speaking of the further negociations at Kotta.

These, so far as it is in my power to report them, will consist mainly, on the side of the Clergy, of resolutions passed in conference at Kotta to be forwarded to the Bishop; and on the Bishop's side, of attempts to find some expedient in the way of compromise, by which, without any abandonment of principle on either side, the final open catastrophe with all its painful consequences of suspended ministrations and flocks unshepherded, might conscientiously be avoided. In either case I copy the texts of the documents from a Colombo paper.

On July 12th, the day after the original interview at Kotta, the following Minute was adopted and sent to the Bishop :—

'The Church Missionaries' Conference having met to consider the communications made to them by the Bishop yesterday, it was resolved—

'1. That the Conference regrets the step taken in writing to a Catechist contradicting the Bishop's orders, previously to communicating with his Lordship; but would respectfully remind the Bishop that it was the unprecedented exercise of authority by him over a lay agent of the Society which gave rise to the step.

'2. The Conference, with feelings of true regret, have to communicate to the Bishop its inability to yield to him the authority he claims over lay agents and congregations connected with the Church Missionary Society, without reference to the parent Committee in London. They would more especially declare their inability to yield to the Bishop the absolute authority in all matters spiritual claimed by him yesterday in the following words: "In spiritual matters the Bishop's word is law, pending an appeal to higher spiritual authority," "even against the decisions of legal courts."

'3. In special reference to the Bishop's action with regard to the Tamil Cooly Mission, the Conference begs to enter its respectful but decided protest, and to record its opinion that, in proposing to transfer its management to other hands, he lays claim to an authority altogether beyond that which his episcopal office confers.

'4. That the members of the Conference, as Clergymen and loyal members of the Church of England, desire to express their adherence to the principles and discipline of that Church as by law established, and their readiness to comply with every requisition of the Bishop of the Diocese which can legally be demanded from them.'

The same day the Bishop enclosed a formal reply to these resolutions in a little note to Mr. Oakley, the Secretary. This is the note:—

'COLOMBO, *July* 12, 1876.

'Dear Mr. Oakley,—

'Alas! there is nothing in your communication of to-day which the least alters the position. I trust that you will find it possible to try some other course; at least let me have an interview here, or at Kotta, as you like, with two or three of you, before matters come to the last extremity. I enclose a formal answer.

'I am spending much of these days in prayer for GOD's blessing on your deliberations.

'Believe me
'Your faithful servant in Christ,
(Signed) 'R. S. COLOMBO.'

And the enclosure was as follows :—

'COLOMBO, *July* 12, 1876.
'Dear Mr. Oakley,—

'I have received a copy of your resolutions.

'1. As to the first, I accept with thankfulness your expression of regret, and quite understand that the surprise felt at an action on my part which, whether right or wrong, was unexpected by you, goes far to excuse the step taken.

'2. The second resolution I regret, as it virtually postpones the Bishop's authority to that of the parent Committee. The latter part obliges me to say that I do not think I used the words quoted as they stand. They appear to be a combination of two separate sentences or answers of mine. They are unmeaning if strictly taken, and in their apparent meaning are probably untrue. I beg therefore to disclaim them, or, if need be, to retract them.

'3. The third resolution requires no reply.

'4. In the fourth resolution, while I value duly your profession of loyalty, I find a very important defect, if I rightly understand it. If by "which can legally be demanded" you mean " which it is not illegal to demand," your words contain an ample recognition of the Bishop's authority; but if you mean " the demand of which can be enforced by law," then I would remind you that the Bishop has an authority of which the law takes no account, and is bound to make demands of spiritual persons which he cannot legally enforce.

'There is, I am sorry to say, nothing in these resolutions which would induce me to cancel the act of yesterday, by which those to whom it referred are incapacitated legally, I believe, as well as spiritually, from exercising spiritual functions in the Diocese.

'I am
'Your faithful servant in Christ,
(Signed) 'R. S. COLOMBO.'

On the next day again, July 13th, a further Minute was sent to the Bishop.

'MINUTE III.

'*July* 13, 1876.

'It was resolved—

'1. That the Conference regrets that the Bishop is unwilling to accept its views as expressed in the resolutions forwarded to him yesterday.

'2. That it is unable to concede anything on the point at issue beyond what was expressed in them.

'3. That under these circumstances, while the Conference will be glad to receive and give due consideration to any communication his Lordship may wish to make to them by letter, it expresses its opinion that another interview would be unlikely to lead to any satisfactory solution of the present difficulty.'

The Bishop, in replying, set before them a suggestion which he greatly hoped would meet the immediate necessity. The point of it was that they should temporarily and under protest submit to his demands during six months; submit, that is, as to demands made and insisted on by the

Bishop; submit under protest as to demands which they regarded as arbitrary and wrong; the meaning of the six months being that there should be full leisure for abundant communications backwards and forwards with the Committee in London. And at the same time, to make all clearer, he sent also a little paper formulating his demands in such manner as to show both their nature and principle.

Here is the Bishop's letter:—

'Colombo, *July* 13, 1876.

'Dear Mr. Oakley,—

'I regret that you are unwilling to grant me an interview. To refuse such a thing to your Bishop is a strange act; and in any case, to decline an interview is to lose an opportunity for adjusting differences much better than can be done by letter. But I will put my advice before you in writing.

'I believe that many of you think yourselves precluded from choice in this matter by your relation with other members of the Church Missionary Society at home or elsewhere. I am ready therefore to give you, if possible, time to consult with them.

'For this purpose I recommend to you the following course, on your adoption of which I will cancel the revocation of your licenses, deferring further action until January, 1877:—

'That after reading the statement enclosed in the paper marked A, you should pass the resolutions on the paper marked B.

'I have now done the utmost I can, and may God give you grace to act according to His will.

'I remain

'Your faithful servant in Christ,

(Signed) 'R. S. Colombo.'

This is accompanied by—

'A. *Statement of claim advanced by the Bishop.*

'*July* 13, 1876.

'I cannot consent to accept candidates for confirmation at the hands of those who will render me no account of the manner in which they have been prepared, or admit my judgment as to the persons by whom they have been prepared, or the places or occasions in which the Holy Communion will be administered to them.

'I cannot give permission for the baptism of adults to those who may have put them for preparation under the care of persons, as to whose fitness and capacity I am not consulted.

'I cannot authorize Clergy to collect and form congregations (especially when the absence of a consecrated church gives no security for their reverent worship and orthodox teaching) unless such congregations are recognized as being subject to my control and authority.

'I desire to place, have placed, and will place, the utmost trust in the Clergy over whom I am set, but I will not surrender my right or ignore my duty to supervise them in such matters as the above, and, if need be, to interfere.

'I claim therefore to be informed, whenever I desire information, of any appointment to any spiritual office, lay or clerical, in the Church, and to have a right of *veto* on the same, and to be informed in all cases where the importance of the matter or my own desire makes it necessary, of all changes in the management, order of service, or place of worship of any congregation.

(Signed) 'R. S. COLOMBO.'

'B. *Resolutions suggested.*

'Having read the Bishop's statement of his claims of

authority over all congregations and all who minister in them ordained or unordained, we resolve,—

'1. That we respectfully reserve our assent to the principles involved, not being convinced that his Lordship's demands are such as his Episcopal authority can warrant.

'2. That with the above promise we undertake for the rest of the current year not to resist or disallow the supervision or interference of the Bishop in the matters mentioned in his statement.

'3. That we will endeavour at once to procure such advice as may guide us to a right decision as to our conduct after the 1st of January next.

'4. That in the meantime we will do all in our power to preserve peace in the Church and to discourage all who would make out of this our present difference with the Bishop a ground of scandal or division.'

This proposal might, the Bishop hoped, meet the necessities of the case. It seemed indeed to be upon a promising line: at another moment it might have answered the purpose. But I need hardly point out how terribly such a form of pacific suggestion, coming at this moment, was prejudiced by what was meanwhile being done,—far more still by that which was supposed to be meant,—in respect of the Cooly Mission.

The formal reply was as follows:—

'MINUTE V.

'*Friday, July* 14.

'Resolved:—1. That some of the claims made in paper A are such as the Missionaries of the Church Missionary Society have never questioned.

'2. That the authority claimed by the Bishop over Catechists, congregations, and places of worship we cannot yield for reasons already given.

'3. That under these circumstances we are unable to sign the resolutions "B" now laid before us.'

And here is the account as given in Mr. Jones' paper:—

'On the 13th of July, two days be it remembered after the licenses had been withdrawn, the Bishop laid before the Conference a written statement of his claims, and certain resolutions which he desired the members to adopt as a condition on which their licenses, with the exception of Mr. Clark's, should be returned. The claims included many the propriety of which the Missionaries had not questioned: such as the right of the Bishop to receive all necessary information as to the preparation of candidates for confirmation, etc.; but at the same time others which, not merely as abstract questions but also in view of the position which the Bishop had adopted in reference to the Tamil Cooly Mission, it was impossible to admit. To allow the right of veto on the appointment of native agents would have at once deprived the Missionaries of all power of protesting effectively against an act which they could not regard otherwise than as one of spoliation.'

So again Mr. Jones, writing on July 17 to his churchwardens, had said of this suggestion of the Bishop's:—

'Had he said "legitimate authority" no one could have thought of declining, but I need not point out that, just at present, it virtually demanded a surrender of the points mentioned above, which, had they been yielded for six months, could never afterwards be maintained.

'It must too in this connection be remembered that the Bishop's action in reference to the Cooly Mission, which has been brought before the public in his circulars, was such as to preclude the possibility of our accepting such terms.'

This overture therefore failed. One other attempt the Bishop made to prevent the full painful results of the suspension from falling upon the congregations. Mr. Jones comments upon this with some severity. If it should seem to any to be a desperate one, then that desperateness is the measure of the urgency of his desire that the results should, by any possibility, be averted. On Friday, July 14th, the day before the suspension was to become final, he went over to Kotta, not after a second request for an interview, but without any notice and unexpectedly. He found the Clergy assembled, and they received him, since he had come. He came with a suggestion intended to be made to them confidentially, (not as altering the situation, but to avoid if possible a specific result which was too painful to be accepted if it were possible to avoid it;)—namely, that even though it should be necessary that the suspension of licenses should openly follow, yet if they continued to carry on their ministrations for the next few weeks or months without license, he would not regard it as an act of defiance, but would accept it as done, for the time at least, in virtue of an understanding with himself, for the sake of minimizing to the Church the necessarily painful effects of the difference which had arisen. But they first declined to accept, under the circumstances, any confidential suggestion: and when the suggestion was consequently made without any reservation or limit as to its publicity, they waived it aside—taking the opportunity which the Bishop had not unconsciously offered in making such a suggestion,—with something like an indignant disclaimer. Subsequently, in the same interview, the Bishop suggested the possibility of now drawing a distinction, and restoring the licenses of all the other Missionaries, except Mr. Clark's (or except Mr. Clark's and Mr. Cavalier's, I am not sure which the suggestion was). The Missionaries in reply to this referred to his treatment of the Cooly Mission, and asked for the complete restoration of that and its officers to their former condition, professing themselves in that case, but only in that case, ready to resume their work. This attempt having also failed, the Bishop returned to Colombo. The Missionaries then passed and forwarded to him the following Minute:—

'MINUTE VI.
'*July* 14, 1876.

'The Church Mission Conference begs respectfully to inform the Bishop that as the license of each and every member of its body was taken away at the same time, on the same grounds, and by means of the same Deed; it feels that it cannot accept the Bishop's offer to restore any one of the licenses withdrawn, unless all named in the Deed are dealt with in the same way.'

To this the Bishop sent an answer the same day:—

'COLOMBO, *July* 14, 1876.
'Dear Mr. Oakley,—

'I have received your communication of this evening. The members of your so-called conference are in error in supposing that all the licenses revoked on Tuesday were revoked on the same grounds. Two of them would have been revoked had I never met you on that day, though for somewhat different reasons. Nor have I at any time recognized the existence of such a "body" as the 'Church

Mission Conference.' As I announced to you on the 11th instant, a separate Deed of Revocation will be sent to each of you in due course.

'I claim of course no right for myself or the other Clergy to enter any of your churches, being unconsecrated; but if anyone among you desires the ministrations of a clergyman in his church, I will do my utmost to provide one, and to ensure that the mode of conducting service shall be such as he would wish.

'Commending you all to the Grace of GOD,
    'I remain your faithful servant in Christ.
          (Signed)   'R. S. COLOMBO.'

Here is Mr. Jones' account of this last negociation:—

'The Bishop then enquired what course the Missionaries would adopt should he see fit to return their licenses? It was replied that if all were returned they would of course resume their duties. The Bishop declined to return all, saying that under no circumstances would he restore Mr. Clark's. The Missionaries felt that they had as a body been dealt with arbitrarily and unjustly, if not illegally, and they therefore respectfully informed his Lordship that they were unwilling to receive back the licenses of any unless all were restored. The Bishop declining to concede this, all negociations ceased.'

In these extracts we see, I think, clearly enough the position of both sides, at the moment when Saturday, July 15th, ended without the discovery of any compromise, and the suspension of the licenses became absolute.

My task is nearly finished now. I have tried to represent as accurately as I could the original position of things in February last, and the development from that to the position of the middle of July. I do not propose to attempt to give a history of all that has been said or done on the subject since; especially as the detail of the sequel soon passes beyond my knowledge. But there are two modifications or alterations of the position of July 15th, which are too essential to be unrecorded.

The first requires comparatively little explanation. It is the restoration of eleven out of twelve of the suspended licenses. They were restored, as is generally known, in deference to the wish of the Bishop of Madras, the acting Metropolitan. But what is not I think as generally known, as in the interests of a right understanding of the whole matter it needs to be, is the real nature of the Metropolitan's communication. When it is reported that the Bishop of Colombo suspended certain licenses on certain grounds, and afterwards restored them, by desire of his Metropolitan, it is naturally inferred that the Metropolitan, after examination of the circumstances and all that they involved, proceeded, if informally yet at least semi-judicially, to reverse the Bishop of Colombo's judgment. But it would be quite a mistake to suppose this. The Bishop of Colombo, very shortly after the events, wrote to acquaint the Metropolitan with what had happened. This he did in the first instance in a short letter, containing the barest possible outline of fact,— rather indeed a notification of results than any explanation of their meaning. To this, and this only, the Metropolitan replied, not of course passing judgment upon the whole case, with which he was not then acquainted, but deprecating strongly the result. Now the Bishop of Colombo in his own mind had always distinguished, as sharply as possible, between two different kinds of things; on the one hand a principle of Church constitution, which he in his sacred office was absolutely bound to maintain, without compromise or shrinking, and which so long as he held that office he dared not concede to anyone: and on the other hand all the detail of his own conduct in defence of that principle. In respect of the whole of this latter, he was ready at any moment,—I could almost say, more ready than enough,—to be told by any competent authority that he was wrong, to be overruled, to be required to reverse his own measures. When, therefore, the Metropolitan wrote, though not officially, though before having heard any of the circumstances,—and very strongly deprecated his mode of procedure, he was quite ready and glad to accept this opinion as condemnation of his method. One license indeed there was which he did not feel at liberty to return. So far as the suspension was capable of being regarded as a trenchant method of vindicating an imperilled principle, necessary (if necessary) as the only accessible or the best method of vindication, but still as a method, able to be dissociated from maintenance of the principle, and to be dispensed with, if the principle were otherwise adequately maintained; so far he felt that the Metropolitan's opinion imposed upon him the necessity of reversing it. But where his act of withdrawal had been both this and more: required not only as the means of asserting a challenged principle, but also by the direct duty of maintaining discipline, there he felt neither compelled nor at liberty to go back from it. There has therefore been no question before him of restoring Mr. Clark's license. The licenses of the ten who had insisted upon coming in, in the second instance, as champions of a principle, he restored at once: and to restore them was mere relief and gladness. He told them, indeed, that this restoration implied no shadow of change in his principle, or his resolution to maintain it; but to be able to tell them this, and hand back the licenses withal; to have given to the principles and sacred order committed to him that terrible emphasis which he had not dared to shrink from giving, yet fully to embrace again and reinstate the individuals; to reinstate them, moreover, through no means which could even be construed as a tottering of his own convictions, but rather such as accentuated, not slurred, the clear lines of ecclesiastical discipline and order; this was a thing to thank GOD for heartily. The eleventh license, that of Mr. Cavalier, whose part had merely been to defer to others, was delayed for a few days; not that its restoration was doubted of, but because the terms in which it should run required some consideration, in reference to the altered state of things. He was then licensed, as a clergyman of the Church Missionary Society, to work on in his old sphere, — bound by no compact, but desired to bear in mind the Bishop's wishes, — pending negociations which the Bishop had opened with the Home Committee of the Society, in respect of the future occupancy of the Tamil Mission. Such were the circumstances of the restoration of licenses. Since that time indeed the Bishop of Madras has received considerable fulness of information as to the whole matter. What his judgment on the matter would be, or will be (if indeed he will now communicate any) I of course cannot tell : but I have not yet heard that he has given utterance to any opinion at all, since he has been put in possession of the case.

The second change of position has been this moment referred to. It is in regard to the future occupancy of the Tamil Mission. I have referred more than once to the introduction of this topic into the question of principle at Kotta ; and always (I hope not unbecomingly) spoken of it as a complication. I believe that it did complicate the more universally important question in two senses : first, as making the nature of the issue harder to understand, more intricate, more involved ; and secondly, as making the Bishop's general position, so far as it was understood, more out of accord with public sentiment, harder to commend to common acceptance, more (at least on the outward face of it) questionable. And I think that the introduction of this matter complicated the question all the more, in both senses, for a further reason. This is that the Bishop's action (as I have partly already explained) did not seem in this matter to be quite consistent with itself. It seemed to proceed upon two principles, to oscillate between two hypotheses, not quite compatible with each other. Let me explain more fully. Suppose the Bishop to be resolved, as on the 11th of July, to disallow the existing Cooly organization, and to reorganize. The old organization meanwhile is there. How and on what principle is he to behave towards it? It will be remembered that there is an ambiguity in its own constitution. In respect of its committee it does not distinctively belong to the Church of England: in respect of its managing Clergy it does,— or did, for at the moment of the hypothesis they are being withdrawn from it. Is then the 'Mission' to be treated as part of the Church of England? If it is, the object will be, so far as is consistent with rights of private property, etc., to influence it, to invite it to take part in reorganization, and, if it will, to incorporate it. If it is not, the nature of the action will be to leave it aside, unrecognized and untouched, and without reference to it to begin new work upon the ground on which it stood. Either of these hypotheses carries a separate form of practical consequence. Either is logical, but the two can hardly be combined. In the old practice there was indeed an ambiguity; that is, there was an attempt to combine two principles not really compatible: and hence a great part of the unsatisfactoriness of the old practice. But in the Bishop's action also there seemed, I believe, to the by-standers to be an ambiguity, a combination of the two hypotheses in the only form in which being inconsistent they could be combined in his action, namely, by an oscillation from the one to the other. In the first instance he was understood to speak and act upon the former hypothesis, and shortly afterwards he seemed to explain himself upon the latter. There was therefore from these causes an additional uncertainty, further complicating what was complicated before, and making the real nature of the Bishop's position and contention the more obscure to the general public.

Now at a very early stage after the moment of crisis the Bishop proposed a course which, if taken up by the Church Missionary Society, would have the effect of clearing these complications out of the way. He proposed to the Home Committee that the field of Cooly Mission work should be occupied by the Church Missionary Society itself, not working as a deputy under an undenominational management, but in its own name. This proposal would supersede the original plan of putting all at once under the Archdeacon. It would replace in the Society's hands (only on sounder terms) what had been in a manner in their hands before. And in part, I doubt not, the proposal was meant as an expression of the Bishop's desire to avoid —even, if necessary, by modifying former action—anything which might be thought exceptionable or unfair. No doubt in offering this, he could not offer to dispense, in this one department of work, with that condition of principle which he was requiring of the Society everywhere: nor could he fail to demand of them now what he had consistently demanded before, that the Chaplains also should be allowed to do Tamil work; so that the offer was necessarily made with three conditions,—first, the general one, that the Society should concede the principle of the subordination of *all* Church Ministers to the Bishop, by allowing him a veto on the appointment of Catechists; secondly, that there should be some real guarantee that the working of the Mission was *bonâ fide* entirely emancipated from the control of the undenominational committee; and thirdly, that the liberty of the Chaplains should be recognized. As the weeks went on, the Bishop was disposed to dwell with the more emphasis upon this plan, looking upon it (more pointedly perhaps than when he first shaped the proposal) as the most important fact in the position at the moment, and rather holding his hand from other beginnings of organization, till he should receive answer about this. I do not suppose that all other beginnings of Tamil work were suspended, if only because in any case it was part of the condition that there should be Chaplains preparing to work, and arranging work under themselves: but there was certainly this change; that whereas at the first moment the Bishop appeared to stand as claiming the whole field of Tamil work to be occupied and arranged under the directest form of Diocesan organization; (and this claim moreover was found to be a prominent stumblingblock in the way of any approach to mutual understanding respecting the principles in question at Kotta;) now the Bishop is offering to delegate that field of work, upon those terms on which alone he feels that any such delegation can be tolerated, to the very much more indirectly 'Diocesan' working of the Church Missionary Society.

NOTE.—Here, too, I have to add that the Church Missionary Society has, since my writing, published resolutions which deprive me of the right of using the present tense, as though any friendly negociations were at this moment in process, in respect of the future arrangement of Cooly work. For the present, it seems, they maintain without qualification of syllable or letter the old condition and management of the Tamil Cooly Mission, together with Mr. Clark and all that he has done. I much regret the position taken up, even though it be regarded as merely a temporary expression of opinion. I can only suppose that the separate organization of Tamil Missionary work in connection with the Chaplains, under the Archdeacon and the Bishop, must quietly proceed meanwhile.

I BELIEVE that I now may end. I know indeed how necessarily incomplete my narrative is, even with the desire to be full. And I know that were it ever so exact as history, the history of what has now happened in Ceylon is but the preliminary to the real question, and its real interest. That question, indeed, cannot be adequately dealt with, till there is knowledge of the events. But it is when they are known that the question begins really to open itself as part of a fundamental question of Church constitution. As a question of Church principle and constitution it is a question of urgent interest to the whole Church. Its thorough weighing and settlement is no offhand matter; it must depend upon Church theory and Church history, both primitive and modern. It is not the first time that the adjustment of Society's management with Church constitution has presented itself as a question in modern ecclesiastical history. Perfect understanding of the question now involved would require considerable acquaintance with the earlier negociations on the same subject. But as Church organization is being developed on all sides,—in the Colonies, at home, and at last, thank GOD! though so tardily, even in India; the settlement of this question presses upon the Church more inevitably—and more instantly. It has been raised in Colombo, not as I believe that it may be settled in Colombo alone, possibly not that it may be settled quite immediately at all; but that it may be settled (I believe) by and for the whole English Church,—and not many years hence,—and finally. It has been raised by the Bishop of Colombo's action, because the necessity of action forced itself on him: and it is probable that it has been raised in the only way in which he could possibly have raised it as a question before the whole Church. It confronted the Bishop within his diocese, and as Bishop of the diocese he met it. It would not have been raised nor met, if as Bishop of the diocese he had bent to the storm, and as an individual protester had addressed his private remonstrance to a private Society's committee-room in London. But it is before the Church now; as very soon, in any case, it must have been. So long as it is open, so long as it is a question, it is no off-hand matter but of the gravest importance. It must be approached and dealt with as a grave question, to be judged by the light of the whole Theory and History of the Church. Yet it may be that the question will hardly be closed, before men will marvel that it was ever a question.

The following extract is from the speech made by the Bishop of Colombo in reply to an address of sympathy recently presented by 1277 laymen of the Diocese, as reported in the 'Guardian' of Nov. 8th. It seems so directly to the purpose as the completion of the history explained above, that I may be pardoned for copying it:—

'You are right in believing that it is for unity that I am contending. In the means I have used, and in my own manner of using them, there may have been much that was wrong; but the main object has certainly been that which was so near to the heart of our LORD, and has always had a foremost place in the prayers of His people,—the Unity of His Church. In England the parochial system is guarded so jealously by law that there is little danger of the existence side by side of rival or independent congregations; but here there is no such security; and the only guarantee against the division of congregations in any place is the reference to a central authority, who may decide under what circumstances a separate congregation may be judiciously allowed. But this local unity is not all that the Church requires. The unit is not the congregation but the diocese; and there must be between the several parts of a diocese—not, indeed, absolute uniformity of plan, but—such co-operation as may constitute it an organized whole. This "coherence" as you have called it, this compactness of organization, can only be ensured by the recognition of a central authority who shall superintend the whole. This central authority is provided by GOD's appointment in the Episcopate; and the Bishop is not merely an officer to perform certain functions, but a head, to represent and maintain the unity of the Church. But the Bishop should assert this unity and maintain these principles not unsupported. He ought not to be denouncing them as if they were his own arbitrary decisions; he should be guided and supported by the advice of his assembled clergy. As it is, the Church's claims must either be unasserted, or they must be asserted by the Bishop on his own responsibility. Thus they have inevitably the appearance of arbitrary decisions and personal claims; they come with but little weight, and easily excite resentment. But were the Bishop properly advised and supported by the presbytery in synod this would not be so. I trust that our recent troubles have made this defect so apparent, that it must soon be remedied; and if they result in a vigorous demand on the part of the laity, that the clergy shall duly gather round their Bishop in synod, then our troubles will not have been borne in vain.'

www.ingramcontent.com/pod-product-compliance
Lightning Source LLC
Chambersburg PA
CBHW020135170426
43199CB00010B/757